Lead Smart, is an insightful book for leaders who want to take their personal productivity, effectiveness and teams to the next level. The book takes the reader on a logical journey with insightful examples and models which can be easily applied to everyday life in a busy leadership role. *Lead Smart* is the perfect book end to Dermot's other work on productivity and a book which can be used ongoing in any leadership journey or team environment.

Mike Boyle,
HP Senior Vice President LF Print WW

In the age of AI this book may the answer to human endeavour.

Matt Church,
founder, Thought Leaders, author, *Rise Up*

With *Lead Smart,* Dermot Crowley again demonstrates his deep understanding of how productivity can impact performance in the corporate workplace, and what leaders can do to maximise productivity for themselves and their teams. This book is a great addition to the body of work Dermot has created to help leaders, managers and workers to get more done in a balanced, effective and productive way.

Susan Ferrier,
Group Executive People & Culture,
National Australia Bank

Whether you are an aspiring leader or already at a senior level, continuing to learn and test yourself is a must. Focusing on your own leadership skills and gaps allows you to not only become a better leader yourself, but also coach and develop the leaders of the future. In *Lead Smart*, Dermot poses the question, just how smart are you leading? Then delivers valuable tools and insight to challenge your current habits and create new ones to understand and address your own leadership potential. An absolute must for leaders of today, tomorrow and the future.

Paul Gracey,
board member and non-executive director

Lead Smart is a must-read for busy leaders seeking practical solutions to boost productivity. Dermot Crowley's insightful book not only offers a wealth of useful tips for leaders but also prompts valuable self reflection. It sheds light on how well-intentioned actions can inadvertently hinder team performance. Personally, investing in this book and Dermot's training has proved invaluable for my own growth, and that of my team. With its impact and depth, *Lead Smart* stands as another powerful contribution by Dermot Crowley.

Martin Paino,
partner, KPMG

Lead Smart is a practical no-nonsense guide for leaders on how their organisations can achieve more in a sustainable way — without the proverbial 'busyness'. As with any important organisational change it does require a lot of 'rewiring' — starting from the senior leaders. But with commitment it makes a huge impact. Having adopted Dermot's approach to improving personal, teams and leader productivity, many in our team refer to it as a 'game changer'.

Maxim Sharshun,
senior executive, Medibank

Amidst a vast ocean of leadership self-help books, *Lead Smart* shines brilliantly as a true game-changer. It skilfully guides leaders to uncover their own hidden workstyle biases that hinder their and their team's performance, setting the stage for remarkable personal and team growth. With practical strategies and a roadmap for action, this indispensable gem is a must-read for leaders and managers who are striving for enhanced productivity and fulfilment in their own work, and that of their teams and organisations.

Betina Szkudlarek,
Professor of International Management,
University of Sydney

Any book linking productivity, leadership and culture is going to catch my attention. Dermot's book, *Lead Smart,* shows us how to shift our team cultures through our own leadership actions and habits. Leaders are looking for cultures that work (or tackling cultures that work against them) and team culture is a great place to start, for what is an organisation except a collection of teams? Regardless of your market, product or maturity, all organisations need to shift beyond bursts of productivity to accountable cultures for true productivity shifts. Dermot's book shows us how to lead our teams through everyday actions (and without the long hours).

Meredith Wilson,
culture strategist, author,
speaker, executive mentor

Dermot Crowley's *Lead Smart* is a game-changer! As a productivity guru, his fourth book delivers practical strategies for leaders to elevate their productivity and drive exceptional results in their teams. Having experienced Dermot's expertise firsthand at Dreamworld, his insights have revolutionized our time management and team effectiveness. While *Lead Smart* will help me continue to work on my own productivity, more importantly, it will supercharge the productivity of our leadership team, and in a global environment where everything is moving faster than yesterday, that matters. A must-have guide for anyone striving to be an exceptionally productive leader.

Greg Yong,
Group Chief Executive Officer,
Ardent Leisure (Dreamworld,
Whitewater World and SkyPoint)

SMART
PRODUCTIVITY

LEAD
SMART

SMART
PRODUCTIVITY

LEAD SMART

How to Build and Lead Highly Productive Teams

DERMOT CROWLEY

WILEY

First published in 2024 by John Wiley & Sons Australia, Ltd
Level 4, 600 Bourke St, Melbourne, Victoria 3000, Australia

Typeset in Crimson Text 12pt/15pt

© John Wiley & Sons Australia, Ltd 2024

The moral rights of the author have been asserted

ISBN: 978-1-394-18860-4

NATIONAL
LIBRARY
OF AUSTRALIA

A catalogue record for this book is available from the National Library of Australia

Cover design by Wiley

Disclaimer
The material in this publication is of the nature of general comment only, and does not represent professional advice. It is not intended to provide specific guidance for particular circumstances and it should not be relied on as the basis for any decision to take action or not take action on any matter which it covers. Readers should obtain professional advice where appropriate, before making any such decision. To the maximum extent permitted by law, the author and publisher disclaim all responsibility and liability to any person, arising directly or indirectly from any person taking or not taking action based on the information in this publication.

Contents

Acknowledgements

As always, writing a book takes a lot of hard work, buckets of coffee and access to tissues occasionally. I always swear I will never do it again, but eventually the siren's call tempts me to do it once more! While most of the work (sketching out ideas) is usually done over a couple of years, the final six to 12 months can be a crazy time as I get my words down on paper, and wrestle with the challenge of creating a unique and meaningful book that adds value to the world, rather than one that just takes up space on a bookshelf. As always, there are a lot of people to thank for their support, encouragement, patience, inspiration and honesty. This is a dedication to them.

To my wife, Vera, who has supported me every step of the way, and provided so much insight into her role as a senior leader. Every time I doubted myself, I looked into her eyes and saw reflected a man who could do anything he sets out to do. She encouraged me to lock myself away and write for weeks at a time, and was always waiting for me on my return with a big kiss. *Grazie, bella.*

To my son, Finn, who has endured me writing four books now, and I suspect, while quietly impressed, still thinks I am on a pretty good wicket, getting paid to write books and speak.

He is right; it is not a bad life. I hope he takes inspiration from me and creates a life by design for himself.

To my sister, Margaret, who is far away in Dublin, but always so proud of me and what I have done. And to Donal, our late brother, who I know would have loved this book.

To my team, Tony, Matt and Chauntelle, who help me bring my ideas to life, and to our clients. You guys are so fantastic.

To my crew at Thought Leaders, who always serve to inspire my thinking, and provide the advice I need when I am stuck.

To Kelly, my editor before my manuscript gets to Wiley, and to all of the Wiley team who work tirelessly to make my words make sense to you, the reader. You might not be able to spot the magic they weave into a book like this, but you would be able to spot it if they didn't.

To my training, speaking and coaching clients, who have provided so many ideas and anecdotes for this book — I have written this with you and the issues you face in mind. I hope it serves you well.

And to you, the reader. We don't know each other yet, but I thank you for at least picking this book up, and hope you enjoy and use its ideas.

Dermot Crowley

Introduction

As a leader, working at or near the top levels of your organisation, your role is leading the troops, setting the strategy and executing the plans. You must have been somewhat organised and productive to get to this level. You have to be efficient and effective, using your time, energy and focus with laser precision to operate successfully as a leader. In fact, your ability to get stuff done would be seen as a critical skill as you rose to your position.

But what if I told you that you may not be as efficient or effective as you think, and you may have attained this position in spite of, rather than because of, your organisation skills?

What if I said that, as a leader, you may be a part of the reason your team struggles with their productivity? Or that your team culture could be working against productivity rather than supporting it?

What if you and your team are incredibly busy, but busy working on the wrong stuff?

What if you are the leader, but are simply too busy to lead effectively?

The path to leadership is a long and often challenging one. We work diligently at school, then possibly spend a few years at university. We get our first job, the first rung on the ladder to be climbed. Over the years, we work hard and develop our skills. We eventually find ourselves in a position where we are managing and leading people. For the select few, you might climb to the pinnacle of senior leadership, and possibly end up as MD or CEO.

Some of us deliberately choose this path, while some of us fall into it. Either way, now that we are here, we want to have an impact. We want to make a difference, lead our teams well and help our organisation to excel. But in the back of our minds, some fears lurk and fester. The fear that we are busy doing lots of activity, but not having the impact that we would like. Or the fear that we are having an impact, but at a cost to our balance, family and life outside of work. Or the fear that if we keep going at this pace, we are going to crash and burn.

For many leaders, the reality is that, now they have achieved what would traditionally be described as career success, they have never felt so busy, so distracted, so overwhelmed and so unable to find time for the things that truly matter in their role. They have never felt so much pressure to stay on top of everything whilst moving at a million miles an hour.

In my work with thousands of leaders over the last 25 years, I have seen a lot of these leaders fall victim to crushing meeting schedules, hopelessly overflowing inboxes, constant interruptions and a sense of busyness that does not equate to effectiveness in their role. Many of these leaders work in large corporates: financial institutions, large consulting firms, multinational manufacturing or retail conglomerates. But this problem is not solely the problem of leaders in large organisations (although, of course, this problem is most likely to exist in these larger companies due to their complexity). This problem can also be seen in medium and even small businesses.

The simple truth is that leaders are often too busy to have the impact that they need to have. But I strongly believe that when we attain a leadership role, we need to become less busy and shift our focus and mindsets from *activity* to *impact*. We need to concentrate our time, energy and focus on the few things that really matter and empower our teams to execute on the right priorities with our direction. We need to protect time to think, to plan, to make good decisions and to provide clear direction. We need to be responsive and available to our team, not constantly unavailable in meetings. And we need time to coach and mentor our people, leveraging their skills, capacity and productivity.

That's a bit of a strong start, isn't it? I haven't given you much time to settle in. Now I know that you are unlikely to be experiencing *all* of the issues listed above, but I am sure you identify with at least some of them. And the good news is, there are things you can do, as a leader with agency, that will make a difference and maybe even change the game for you.

Lead Smart is the third of a trilogy of books that I have written on productivity in the corporate workplace. My vision was always to start with the individual, and to present a framework to maximise personal productivity. *Smart Work* serves that purpose. The next step was *Smart Teams*, which explores how we can work together more productively, and minimise what I call 'productivity friction' by creating more productive cultures within our teams.

This is the final piece of the puzzle, where I address the specific productivity issues faced at the leadership level. But to round this trilogy off fully, this book needs to go beyond tactical productivity strategies for leaders. It needs to sound a clarion call to leaders to level up their own productivity, as well as leverage the productivity of everyone around them. To step up to this worthy task, leaders need to put personal and team productivity front and centre of their priorities, to pay attention to it, and work on it every single day.

While the value in this book is not dependent on having read the other books in the series, you will find I do refer to strategies in these other books where relevant. If you want to dig deeper, a read of *Smart Work* and *Smart Teams* would not be a bad idea.

Productivity: A core strand in the leadership rope

Productivity, at least personal productivity, is a topic for discussion for many leaders, but most leaders do not do anywhere near enough work to ensure they and their teams can operate at the highest levels of effectiveness. Productivity is often seen as a minor strand in the complex rope that is leadership.

A cable-laid rope is a large rope typically made of several multi-strand smaller ropes twisted together to form a tight, virtually waterproof cable that is incredibly strong and durable. It was, and in some cases still is, used on ships, where keeping the rope from getting wet is desirable to avoid it getting too heavy to pull out of the water.

A leadership role is like a multi-strand rope, with many different skillsets that combine to make an effective leader, from strategy to motivation to decision-making. I see productivity as one of these strands. A leader must be personally productive and must also work to maximise the capacity of their team to produce great work.

What could be more central to a leader's role than increasing the **capability** *and* **capacity** *of everyone that they work with?*

I worry, though, that productivity is only seen as a minor strand in the leadership rope, surrounded by and lost amongst the more prominent strands associated with a leader's role. I urge you to shift your thinking on this, and see productivity as a core strand. What could be more central to a leader's role than increasing the capability and capacity of everyone that they work with?

It is often assumed that people will be naturally productive or will learn on the job to work effectively. But in today's busy, fast-paced and noisy workplace, productivity cannot be assumed. The productivity strand in a leader's rope needs to be actively developed with purpose and care. If it is not, our rope begins to fray and split, making it weak and at risk of breaking.

I don't pretend to be able to advise you on every strand of your leadership rope. I am not a leadership expert, but I do know productivity, and have worked with many thousands of leaders over the last 25 years. I believe I understand the challenges they face in maintaining effectiveness. I have worked in many industries and businesses, and the productivity cultures that drive these organisations. I have seen firsthand the impact unhealthy productivity cultures have on their people, and the role that leaders play in allowing these cultures to exist.

I believe that there is so much a leader can do to gain more control over what sometimes feels like a chaotic and uncontrollable workplace culture. But unfortunately, a leader's approach to productivity, even if it is solid and organised, is often a reactive approach to productivity. By this, I do not mean that you are reactive rather than proactive, but rather your approach to productivity has been shaped in part as a reaction to your work, your culture and your environment. Next-level productivity requires the leader to shape their own approach to productivity, one that better serves themselves, their team and everyone around them. To be a highly productive leader, you need to demonstrate a sense of agency in a demanding and busy workplace. You need to make productivity a priority, and work at it tirelessly, knowing that the payback will be immensely worthwhile for you and those around you.

Your leadership rope can serve as a tool to lift others up to a higher level, or to tie them up, frustrating their efforts and keeping them down. Let us work together to achieve the former!

What specific problems are we solving?

When we lead productivity, we should experience a productivity gain for ourselves and our team. Ideally, we want this productivity gain to be sustained over a long period of time, not just for a few weeks or months. The challenge is that no matter how high the initial gain is, over time, productivity friction wears away at it until we revert back to a lower level of productivity (see figure A, overleaf).

As we will explore a little further on, productivity friction is often caused by busyness, urgency, disorganisation and distraction. These frictions operate like brakes on our team, diminishing their capability and their output. The good news is, these are all productivity issues that can be managed with a bit of focus and effort. The friction they cause may be hard to totally erase, but it can be minimised.

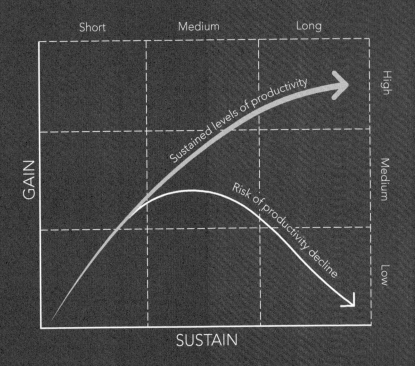

Figure A: The gain/sustain curve

I would love to promise you the equivalent of perpetual motion and say that there is a way to increase productivity forever in your team, but that would be a lie. But I believe you could achieve a significant gain, *and* you could reduce the friction so that the gain is sustained for longer.

To achieve the initial productivity gain, we need to develop productivity skills and capability across our team. To sustain this gain over time, we need to reduce the productivity friction our team has to deal with.

Let's have a look at the four big disrupters of productivity in most workplaces.

The four big productivity disrupters

Busyness. Urgency. Disorganisation. Distraction. As I write about the productivity issues I see dominating most workplaces, I am reminded of the Four Horsemen of the Apocalypse, the allegorical figures commonly known as Pestilence, War, Famine and Death, whose arrival signals the end of the world. That's grim, but maybe not a bad analogy to describe how we sometimes feel when faced with many of the productivity problems that come our way each day, getting in the way of the impactful work we want to achieve.

I like the idea that the Four Horsemen got sick of dealing with the world in general, and decided it was a good bet to niche on the corporate world, transforming into the productivity disrupters of Busyness, Urgency, Disorganisation and Distraction. More fun to be had, and more money to be made in the corporate world!

Every day they move through our workplaces, causing disruption and chaos. Each has their own unique talent, and each causes its own unique form of unproductiveness for you and your team.

Busyness

Many of us feel there is just too much to do, and only so much time, energy and focus to go around. Busyness at the senior level is part of the job description, but if our busyness is caused by poor priority choices or a perceived lack of control in our role, it can have a damaging effect on our work, our team and our combined wellbeing. In the Four Horsemen analogy, busyness is represented by Pestilence, which seems quite fitting. Busyness is like one of the viruses we see in zombie movies on TV, or have experienced with COVID — viruses that are ever-present, contagious, lurking just around the corner, never letting us catch our breath.

Circumstances, and other people, cause us to be busy. But we also feed into the problem by not managing our work well, or by making poor priority choices. Busyness can also be a comfortable mindset that we adopt, almost absolving us from blame when we cannot do everything on our plate. When someone tells me they were too busy to do something, I suspect the reality is they made a choice to focus on other priorities. This is fine if they were informed choices, but sometimes they are not — it's just Busyness doing its sinister work. Some signs of busyness are:

- lack of/unclear priorities

- a need for perfectionism

- lack of alignment

- no time to plan

- reactive workstyle.

Urgency

Coming up behind on a black horse is Urgency, always impatient, always in a hurry, always causing stress and anxiety as he passes. Much of the urgency and reactivity that derails our day is avoidable, and is the direct cause of someone else's poor planning or, shock horror, our own poor planning. I believe urgency to be one of the most insidious forms of productivity disruption in today's workplace. In fact, I wrote a whole book on this topic because of the disruptive power that urgency holds.

In many organisations, urgency has become the dominant way that work is prioritised. People will say that something is important, but what they usually mean is that it is urgent. And urgency rules the day! Workers are often rewarded for being highly responsive, when, in fact, they are just plain reactive. We need to change the script on urgency, and help our team get back to a more importance-driven way of working.

Some signs that urgency holds too much sway are:

- leaving work until the last minute

- being driven by email and instant messages

- an 'I need everything now' culture

- firefighting mindset

- unclear/uncommunicated deadlines.

Disorganisation

Our own disorganisation, and the disorganisation of the people around us, can cause immense frustration and disruption. We forget things, we lose things, we double book things, we don't deliver as agreed, we have to redo things, we get stressed and delete things...you know the feeling. And, of course, our productivity is impacted when other people do all of the above, even though we may be highly organised. Disorganisation is everywhere, and like famine, incapacitates people and their ability to thrive.

Most people have some organisation system in place, but it is often one that has been cobbled together over a number of years, and it kind of works and it kind of doesn't. Our organisation systems are often fragmented, half-baked and not fit for purpose when it comes to staying organised at the leadership level.

Signs of disorganisation are:

- things slip through the cracks
- not being responsive to your team/colleagues
- missing or being late to meetings
- too many ineffective organising tools or lists
- losing track of notes and information.

Distraction

And then there is good old Distraction, bumbling up behind on his stubborn pony, constantly disappearing down rabbit holes and getting stuck in useless bushes. Our own distraction has become more and more problematic as computers, handheld devices, emails and social media have become the norm in our workplaces. Our ability to stay focused on what is important is getting harder, and it's problematic when you look at this phenomenon at a team level. We are distracted on a wholesale level!

There is a whole body of research on distractions in the workplace, and much of it points to the fact that our work is suffering as a result of constant interruptions. Some reports suggest it can take up to 20 minutes to recover from an email distraction. What is this doing to the quality of our work, not to mention our wellbeing? (As a sidenote, I am laughing as I write this because my partner, Vera, has just come in to interrupt me, showing me a house that has sold in our area on her phone. The irony!)

Signs of distraction are:

- constant interruptions

- email alerts not suppressed

- procrastination

- a need for instant gratification

- an inability to deeply focus.

Believe me, Busyness, Urgency, Disorganisation and Distraction are alive and well in your workplace. They are possibly peering over your shoulder right now, ready to compromise your productivity yet again.

If you think about your own personal productivity, which of these disrupters is the biggest handbrake for your productivity? If you consider your team, which is most problematic for them? Do you see these horsemen riding through the halls of your organisation creating havoc?

I'm all in, but how do we do this?

I have framed this book around you, and the people you work with every day (see figure B). This includes your direct reports, your wider team, your peers, and stakeholders in other teams in the organisation. Productivity is all about people, and if you look at how you organise work through a people-focused lens, you will be more likely to build productive habits, ways of working with others and even more productive cultures. The starting point is to examine your own personal habits, mindsets and behaviours.

So, the first part of the book, Yourself, is all about you and how you work. We will talk about the common issues faced by leaders when managing their personal productivity, and why the systems and strategies that got you to this point of your career will no longer cut it. You need to go 'next level' with your personal productivity, and operate with an elite mindset when organising, prioritising and planning. This is not just for your benefit, although you will benefit massively. If you are going to lead productivity successfully in your team, you need to lead by example, so this is an obvious starting place.

Part II, Team interface, will examine how you work with your core team, and how to avoid the productivity friction that may be generated by you, or by them, whenever you interact. Every time you delegate work, have a one-on-one discussion, send an email, collaborate on a project or interrupt with a question, there is a risk that someone's time, energy or focus is going to suffer. But when you learn to work with your team in a way that promotes flow rather than friction, you become a more leveraged leader, enhancing the productivity of those around you. When you coach your team to work and interact with you

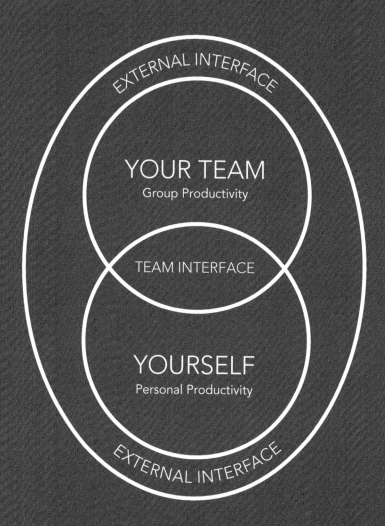

Figure B: Lead Smart framework

in the most effective manner, you make life easier for yourself. The productivity partnerships that are created serve to lift the productivity of all involved.

In Part III, Your team, we explore how you as a leader can build and lead more productive team cultures that benefit your wider team. This is a highly leveraged strategy that ensures that even when you are not involved, your team are enjoying the benefits of working in a team culture that allows them to get on with their most impactful work with the minimum productivity friction. This is how you sustain high levels of productivity over time. Culture is just a set of group behaviours, and your team's behaviours around communications, meetings, collaboration and urgency need to be exemplary. Many leaders like to give their team free rein around how they work and organise themselves, and I, too, believe in allowing people to work according to their preferences — up to a point. When the performance of the individual or the team is impacted by poor productivity practices, the leader needs to step in, set expectations, and set an example to provide the right support and skills to bring productivity up to a reasonable level.

In Part IV, External interface, we will explore how you and your team work with the other teams and stakeholders around you. There is a wider context within which you operate, and your productivity or your team's productivity must be managed within this context. If we do not consider this wider group in our thinking, we will develop productivity strategies in a siloed way, and will not serve the organisation as well as we should.

While you and your team need to work productively with others. I am also very aware that the productivity of your team can be compromised by those outside of your team, and they need to be able to minimise the negative impact of this.

Learning to negotiate workloads and deadlines will help reduce this friction.

Finally, as a leader, I believe that you have an opportunity to create ripples across your organisation that inspire everyone you work with to lift their productivity game. This can inspire your peers to create more productive cultures within their team, and this, again, will help your team, as much of the productivity friction they experience comes from interaction with other teams. As a leader, you have a social responsibility to create a better culture across your organisation if this is within your means, and it will be, believe me.

My desire with this book is to help exceptionally productive leaders lead exceptionally productive teams. This book contains several months of writing, over four years of thinking and more than 25 years of experience working with leaders like you. I am so excited to help you to be the most productive leaders you can be!

Reflections and intentions

- What do you see as the most significant productivity issues facing you and your team?

- What initiatives have you already put in place to maximise productivity?

- Are you committed to concentrating your time, energy and focus on increasing productivity across your team?

PART I
YOURSELF

A friend of mine, Cameron Schwab, spent many years working in leadership roles in Australian Rules Football (AFL) clubs. He was the CEO of three clubs over a period of 25 years: Richmond, Melbourne and Fremantle. For any non-Australians reading this, that is a bit like being CEO of Manchester United, Liverpool and Leeds United in English football! He has seen a game or two of AFL, and been around many players and coaches.

Over a beer one day, we had a chat about a term that is used a lot in the world of sport: 'elite'. He reckons that most players, even at the top level of football, are not elite, even though they think they might be. Any club would be lucky to have one, two, maybe three elite-level players. Now, that is not to say he doesn't think the other players are any good, or that they don't deserve to be there. They are enormously talented, incredibly fit and among the best footy players, but they are not elite.

The few that he would class as elite are the ones who are still on the field practicing their kicks an hour after everyone else has hit the shower. They are the ones who dig deep for that last lung-busting run towards the end of the last quarter. They are the ones who can step up to the big moments and win games when it really matters. A part of what makes them elite is talent and skill, but much of it is their mindset, and the work they put in, day after day, to be the best.

The same is true with productivity. Many leaders who work at the highest levels of their organisations believe that they operate at elite levels of productivity. But the truth is most are not elite. Their productivity is good, reasonable, acceptable. But it is not elite. That label should be kept for the few who work at their productivity skills every day to be the most effective they can be. It should be kept for leaders who work to create highly productive cultures, free of the productivity friction that makes life hard for their teams. It should be kept for the leaders who champion productive ways of working across their team and their organisation.

In all my years of working with leaders in organisations, I have come across a few leaders who have achieved elite levels of productivity. But only a few. I have come across many who would aspire to achieve this, but simply get too busy to do the work required. And I have come across too many who pay lip service to productivity, and bumble their way through their career in an ineffective way that seems to be good enough, but comes at a cost to their wellbeing, and the stress of those around them.

I mean what I have just said with the greatest respect. You may be in one of the latter groups, and feeling a bit disgruntled. But this is one of a few uncomfortable truths I have to share in this book if it is going to be of service.

Productivity is not just how much you produce

For many years, even though I was a supposed expert in the field of productivity, I believe I had a fairly narrow view of what productivity was. In simplistic terms, I saw productivity as how much you produced in the course of your work. I suppose, in that framework, I would have seen elite productivity as a level of productivity that produced more in the time available. Not wrong, but I think it is more useful if we look at productivity in a more nuanced and holistic way.

I had a conversation with a client a couple of years back that changed my thinking of what elite productivity might look like. The client asked me to run some training for their team, but they asked me *not* to call it productivity training, and *not* to use the term 'improving productivity'. I was initially perplexed at this, as I had always positioned our training as training that improved productivity. But after a bit of explorative discussion, I began to see their perspective. They did not want their passionate but very busy workers to feel like management wanted more from them. I realised that their workers' definition of improved productivity was to produce more, and I could see how that might be problematic.

This forced me to think deeply about what I really meant when I talked about improving productivity. My realisation was that productivity needed to be sustainable, and in order to be sustainable, it needed to be discussed in more than just the narrow frame of how much work we produce. I now find it more useful to talk about elite productivity in the following, more holistic way. Increased productivity is about:

- **Control:** When we achieve elite productivity, we feel like we are in control of our work, our time and our priorities. This means that we have a sense of agency, and are not just a victim of the insistent demands of our workplace.

- **Focus:** We have the ability to focus on the things that deserve our focus. We can zoom our focus in and out, keeping the bigger picture in view whilst being able to zoom in and deeply focus on specific issues or elements as needed.

- **Efficiency:** We are able to work in a highly efficient way, using our time, energy and focus to get things done quickly and without friction. We enjoy the benefits of this efficiency, but so do others as we work in a way that does not cause friction for those around us.

- **Impact:** Elite productivity also means we spend more of our time, energy and focus on the things that really have impact. We are not just busy, we are effectively busy. We prioritise ruthlessly, and we work in alignment with our team and peers.

- **Proactivity:** We are not reactive, we are proactive in planning and organising our work, and responsive to the needs of those around us. We dial down the urgency in our world, and encourage those around us to work with a proactive mindset.

- **Balance:** And we do all of this in a balanced way that protects our sanity, wellbeing and health. We work balanced hours; we have balanced schedules; we use our time, energy and focus in a balanced way.

So, as we take your personal productivity to the next level, think about it in this more nuanced, holistic way. It is not enough to produce more at the expense of your work/life balance, your health or even the wellbeing of your team. Elite footy players have the total game—they are fast, they can kick, they are strategic, they are a leader on the field. So elite productivity requires you to be in control, focused, efficient, impactful, proactive and balanced.

Next-level productivity

To get to an elite level of productivity, most people need to jump at least one, if not more, levels. This might seem daunting. Next level is more than implementing a few strategies that may only last a few months. Next level suggests a complete re-engineering of your operating system, a reinvention of the way you work, and the way you interface with your team. What would that take? What would that look like? Is that even possible?

One of my favourite recording artists is the UK singer-songwriter David Gray. I first heard David Gray sing at midnight on 1 January 2000, literally the minute we turned over into a new millennium! I distinctly remember being back in Ireland on holiday, at a millennium party at my brother's house. As everyone else watched the fireworks in the distance from the garden, I wandered into the living room, where a millennium concert was playing on TV. I saw this guy I had never heard of playing his hit 'Babylon', and was blown away.

His backstory is amazing, and a great example of someone going next level. In 1998, he had released three mildly successful albums, but was struggling to cut through in a time when grunge ruled, and singer-songwriters were not in fashion. He got to a point where he had very little money, and was considering giving it all up and getting a real job. But he looked deep inside and asked himself if he could write a better song, write a better album. He gave it one last shot, this time striving to go next level. He and his band locked themselves away in his small Stoke-Newington terrace, and wrote the album *White Ladder*. In fact, most of the album was recorded in his bedroom on basic equipment.

They had 5000 CDs pressed, and took a punt on releasing the album in Ireland, where he had a bit of a following. It was a slow burn, but eventually the album took off, got some airplay in the US, and became a worldwide hit, selling over 7 million copies. It was definitely 'next level', and set David Gray on the path to success, as well as inspiring many singer-songwriters to follow in his footsteps.

I can only imagine that to go next level like that, Gray needed to not only learn a new way of writing, but to actually undo his old way of writing. He would have had to examine everything that he believed about the art of songwriting, and work out what served him and what did not. He would have had to get really clear about what next level looked like, and work out the blockages that were in his way of getting there.

I believe that we need to go through the same cleansing fire to achieve next level with our productivity. Most of us have been working for years without thinking too hard about how we organised ourselves. We created bad habits that did not serve us, and were unaware of better habits that could revolutionise how we worked.

It is never too late to go next level with your productivity. Habits can be broken. New systems put in place. New skills learned and new technology adopted. My advice, and in some ways my whole intent with this book, is to encourage you not to do this alone. Take next-level productivity on as a project for yourself and for your team. You will find it easier to do if those around you are aligned with the new way of working. And believe me, if you are struggling, so are they, so why not work together achieve that sustained productivity gain?

CHAPTER 1

Know your productivity style

Our productivity, or our capacity to produce work, is more than simply our ability to manage time. Time management was a concept that came to the fore in the sixties and seventies, when time and motion studies attempted to revolutionise the efficiency of office workers. Time management training became the buzz, and even today, we still refer to how we organise ourselves within the context of managing time.

Of course, they were not wrong in focusing on how we manage time. It is probably our most precious resource, as once it's gone, it's gone forever. To be productive we need to manage our time very purposefully and carefully. But time is but one of the limited resources we need to manage. We will focus a lot on time management strategies in future chapters, and you will see that the key to managing time well is managing all of the activities that you need to do, both meetings and priorities, within the context of time. But managing the resource of time is not enough.

A second limited resource we need to manage is our energy. We only have so much energy to give to things, and some of our work, and some people, drain more energy than other tasks and people. Some work requires high levels of energy, such as key meetings or presentations, whereas some work needs lower levels of energy, such as processing emails. We all have an energy cycle as we go through the day, with points of high energy and points of low energy. I am a morning person so have the highest energy for complex, creative work first thing in the morning.

When we are full of energy, we can bring a lot to the table. We can do and achieve so much. The quality of our work and our thinking is better. If managing a good system is critical to time management, energy management requires us to manage flow, making sure we have the right levels of energy for the right moments in our week. Key meetings, presentations, negotiations all require the optimal level of energy.

Finally, the third limited resource at our disposal is our focus, or our ability to concentrate on issues, topics and ideas. There are only so many things that we can turn our gaze to in our day. Our attention is sometimes referred to as 'bandwidth', and our bandwidth has a saturation point, beyond which we just cannot absorb any more. To be focused, I believe we need to manage our environment, creating and protecting space for our thoughts and attention.

The resource of time is an external resource that we operate within. Energy and attention are internal resources that we apply to the available time (see figure 1.1).

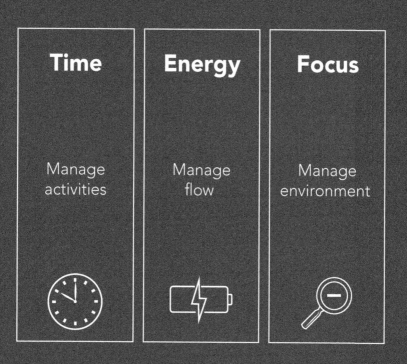

Figure 1.1: Our productivity resources

Your productivity bias

Your time, energy and focus are your personal resources necessary to getting work done. But they are not limitless, and each is best used in the right way at the right time. The challenge we face with these three resources, besides the fact that they are finite, is that we often have a bias toward one or another of these resources, and we tend to lean on that resource too much of the time. This can be a strength, but it can also be a weakness, and it can make us a less effective leader in the long run. The most effective leaders can harness and use all three of these resources in a balanced way.

It may come as no surprise to you, especially if you are familiar with my other books on productivity, that I see myself as pretty organised. I manage my time obsessively, and structure my days and weeks with great care. I don't think this bias for organisation is necessarily in my DNA. I can't remember being particularly orderly as a child, and certainly as a young adult living in a flat with my mates, I was extremely disorganised and messy at times. Organisation is something that I have been exposed to through my career as a trainer after immigrating to Australia, and I have found over time that being organised actually suits me quite well.

I can be pretty black and white about things at times, and for a very long time, as I was teaching my concepts on productivity, I thought everyone was highly organised like me, or if not, they should be. I suppose I have been on a mission for many years to convert people to my way of thinking, which became the Smart Work approach to productivity. But two things happened in 2021 that gave me pause for thought, and became a central inspiration for this book.

The first happened while I was cooking dinner. My passion outside of work is cooking, and I am rather a good cook, if I do say so myself. But I am a recipe cook, not a free-form, make-it-up-as-you-go cook. I need to follow a recipe, and when I do, I can create great meals.

One day I was cooking something that I had cooked before, but only once or twice. I found myself moving from the recipe to the stove, and then back to the recipe again. I would look at the next couple of steps, but as soon as I turned to the stove, I lost my train of thought about what was next, and I had to refer to the instructions again. Something clicked in my brain, and I realised that this was something I had experienced all of my life. I have always struggled to hold information, steps or lists in my head for any length of time. And it was not just recipes. I struggle with directions without my GPS. I struggled at school remembering facts and dates, even though teachers said I was highly intelligent. My mate Nick can tell you who won the third round of the game between the Sydney Swans and the Pies (Aussie sporting enemies) in 2014, yet I struggle to remember the result of last week's game. And when it comes to being organised, I struggle to remember the things I need to do, so have built a methodology around systems to organise my thoughts and actions.

Your time, energy and focus are your personal resources necessary to getting work done. But they are not limitless, and must be managed carefully.

I am not alone in this, and I am sure a number of you identify with this also. I realised that some people could hold this sort of information in their head more easily. Some people can just look at a recipe and off they go without another look. Some people can look at the map and not need to again. Some people can remember a lot of things that they need to do without creating a to-do list. But not me. That was learning number one, a very useful insight into the way I am wired.

I am very lucky to have many brilliant people in my life that inspire my thinking, and two of them are Matt Church and Lisa O'Neill, and through them I came to learning number two. Matt is the founder of an organisation and community called Thought Leaders, and Lisa is the CEO. Thought Leaders is a community of trainers, facilitators and coaches that I have been a part of for coming up on ten years, and it's so important to me that I have become a mentor in that community, working with others to help them build their practices.

As the COVID-19 pandemic raged all around us in 2021, Matt asked me to help run a small workshop in Sydney for some of the community. I was thrilled at the opportunity to get into a room with people again after a couple of years of online delivery, so jumped at the chance. I was a bit out of my comfort zone, as this presentation was not related to the content that I usually delivered on productivity, but Matt and Lisa trusted my experience and ability.

We had a meeting to discuss the day, and the role each of us would play. I went away with some good ideas around how I could add value, and being the organised planner that I am, scheduled some time and actions to get prepared for the day. I created session plans, group exercises, tools and resources — you name it. My sessions were going to be awesome. I like being organised.

On the day, I was a bit nervous. Lisa was a whirlwind of activity, and Matt was his usual composed self. We had a great day with the group, and I felt the pieces I had organised were good enough (not great, though). At the end of the day, myself, Lisa and Matt had a quick debrief. I was exhausted from an intense day. Lisa, I noticed, was full of energy, even after the intensity. I was feeling like my contribution was OK, but when I thought about how Lisa performed through the day, she nailed it. Matt asked me how I felt I had gone. I said good, but felt I had not hit the mark fully. He agreed, and shared with me what he saw happening. This was such an important insight for me, and one that only has positive learning in it.

'The challenge for you Dermot, was that you managed your *time* to prepare for the session', Matt said. 'Lisa, on the other hand, managed her *energy*. Some training sessions require a lot of preparation, but this one needed less organisation and more energy.' I thought about this, and knew he was right. This was a facilitated session to help students create breakthroughs, rather than a training session delivering skills. Lisa shone on the day because she did not spend all of her time leading up to the session doing things. She managed her energy and made sure she was in a space where she could share her energy with the room from a full reservoir. In fact, the night before the session, as I put finishing touches to my training materials, she had booked a spa treatment and a massage. Now I know most people reading this book won't be trainers or facilitators, but I think the learning here has universal application. Sometimes we need to push through by managing time, and sometimes we need to push through by managing energy.

I later reflected on how Matt approached the day. He is a highly experienced speaker, trainer and facilitator, and as I thought about it, I realised he operated in a different way to both myself and Lisa. He sat and watched, he read the room and saw what people needed. He then provided the right solution in the moment, like a surgeon stepping in and performing the perfect cut and stepping back again. This was a different approach again. I managed my time, Lisa managed her energy and Matt managed his focus. I would even go so far as to say that Matt operated at another level altogether, moving between managing his time, his energy and his focus as needed. He had achieved what I believe all leaders need to master, the ability to put the appropriate resource front and centre when needed, and to have the self-awareness to know how you are operating in any moment.

There was something in these realisations that generated the seed for how great leaders need to operate, and in the fact that not everyone is like me, with a bias for managing my time. Indeed, not everyone should be like me — all of the time. Next-level productivity requires us to understand our own productivity preferences and to develop them, but to also strengthen other areas so that we can manage our time, energy or focus as required.

Armed with my insight about my inability to hold information in my head, and this insight about my productivity style, I have expanded my thinking on what productivity looks like, and how harnessing the power of time, energy and focus can lead to greater levels of productivity. I have personally pushed myself to work on my ability to manage my energy and focus more, which complements my ability to manage time.

This is a much richer, more rounded approach to productivity. I have since concluded that these three productivity preferences align to three archetypes. Some leaders have a bias, like me, to organise themselves with the resource of time. Other people get a huge amount of stuff done by harnessing and concentrating their energy, like Lisa. I also believe there is a third group of people who concentrate their focus to get through their work. This last archetype is probably a minority group, but there are definitely people who are not that organised in a time sense, and don't necessarily bring lots of energy to their work, but their superpower is that they can focus deeply on problems or topics in a highly productive way.

Of course, we cannot be too black and white about these things, and just put everyone into neat boxes. You may look at this and conclude that you organise your time really well, but you also manage your energy well. Or you may identify with using energy to push work forward most of the time, but you back it up with good organising skills. Or you identify with focus and time. There is no right or wrong, no judgement, just useful observations. Most people are likely to have a primary bias, backed up by a secondary preference.

To make it easier to describe the attributes for these three archetypes, I am going to call these three groups of people *Organisers, Energisers* and *Analysers.* Don't read into these labels too much though, they are just meant to provide a useful way to talk about each group, and remember, we are all a bit of a mix. If I suggest that you don't use energy as your primary resource for getting work done, I am not suggesting that you are a person without energy. This is a specific context that I hope will help you understand yourself, your behaviours and your blockages better.

The Organisers: Those who have a bias towards time

Organisers choose time as their main productivity resource and preference. When faced with a piece of work, their catchcry is: *'Let's plan this!'* They are organised, they like structure, they make lists and they love a schedule. Their world is orderly, and they invest time in organising their world. They embrace the cutting-edge organising tools of the day. In the 1980s, they would have used a diary and a journal. In the 1990s, they would have loved the Filofax or equivalent. In the 2000s, they got a PalmPilot and started playing about with electronic organising platforms on their 3-inch-thick laptop. In the present day, they fully embrace Office 365 or the Gmail suite. And they read lots of books on productivity methodologies, such as *Getting Things Done* or *Smart Work*. Of course, that is probably at the extreme end of the Organiser spectrum. Many Organisers are a lot more tame, and just like to be organised and manage their time, priorities and information well.

Organisers tend to use structured lists to keep track of the things they need to do. They keep their email inbox well under control, and like to keep their filing systems shipshape and Bristol fashion. They don't tend to rely on their brain to remember stuff, but choose to write stuff down and instead free up their brain to think, plan and create.

They plan their week, and even their day, as a part of their routine. They like to be proactive and plan ahead so that there are no nasty surprises for them or their team. In fact, when an Organiser is placed under pressure to deliver something, or they start feeling stressed and overwhelmed by their work, they put a plan in place. This usually settles them, and helps them to move forward.

They are prepared for meetings, and expect others to be too. They protect time in their schedule for other priorities, so are careful not to give all of their time to meetings. They are responsive to emails and incoming requests, without being reactive. As I write, I realise I am able to detail this way of working very easily as I am an Organiser, and I love to work this way.

People generally like working with Organisers, as they can rely on them to deliver as promised, and know that things won't be forgotten. There are few nasty surprises with Organisers, and because of their planned approach, they get a lot done in the time they have available.

Organiser strengths recap:

- organised schedule and priorities

- good with email management

- clear about priorities

- things don't slip through the cracks

- always able to access the necessary information

- usually good with technology

- prepared for meetings

- work proactively.

But Organisers face some challenges, and have weaknesses like anyone else. They could be accused sometimes of relying on their lists, their schedules and their structure too much. They can get caught up in working their system, and don't always open up to a more flexible approach when necessary. They can consume too much time keeping things organised, rather than just getting on with the work.

Other people who are not organised in the same way (people with a bias for energy or focus) can frustrate them, especially when their work styles impact negatively on the Organiser's work. They get frustrated having to chase people up, and are incredulous when they see how messy other people's inboxes or schedules are. They don't believe that people can get work done effectively if they are not an Organiser.

Sometimes Organisers frustrate other people, especially their team, because they set their expectations too high. They don't always empathise with the fact that everyone has their own way of working. And they can become hard to catch if you need a moment of their time. If you are not in their plan, you may not get a look in.

Organisers who have an EA or PA will usually have a strong relationship with them, working closely with them to stay on top of things. But they can sometimes retain too much control of their own schedule, and don't delegate enough power to their EA. In fact, Organisers can be at risk of not delegating enough to their team, and become overwhelmed trying to do too much themselves.

Organiser challenges recap:

- can be too reliant on their system
- can fall into the trap of just ticking things off their list
- can get stressed if things do not go to plan
- expectations of others can be high
- can be seen as inflexible
- like to maintain control.

If you identify with the Organiser archetype, you possess a skill that takes many people years to master. Being organised is a great foundation for success, and when it is supported by energy and focus, it is even more powerful. It is worth working on the relevant skills and strategies throughout the book that will enhance these parts of your game, especially those parts that talk about organising systems. Remember, the key to managing time is to manage all of your activities within this context.

You may also like to think about how you interact with your team and external stakeholders. Being an Organiser, as we have discussed, can place an unreasonable burden on those around you, so think about the biases or preferences your team have for productivity, and how you can best work with them to achieve the results you need to.

Tips for managing the resource of time

If you want to make sure you are managing the resource of time effectively, especially if you have a bias for energy or focus, you need a system. For me, having a trustworthy system that helps you to manage all of the things that need to be done is critical. Your head is not that system, or at least it shouldn't be. Use a calendar to manage your meetings, and an effective task list to manage your priorities and tasks.

Managing time is also about managing actions, or at least managing the actions that need our attention within the context of time. When planning your week, it is worth taking note of what needs your time across the week, and to think about what you are going to do when. To do this effectively, you need a system that makes all of your actions visible, and that means both your meetings and your priorities should be visible in the same system, and managed in a balanced way (we discuss this in chapters 2 and 3).

Take a systematic approach to email, and keep your inbox under control. Don't just let your emails pile up in your inbox, with no real thought about what needs your attention and when you are going to get to those emails. That approach leads to a reactive way of working, which causes you and others unnecessary stress.

People who have a bias for energy or focus often tell themselves that they are just disorganised and can't get on top of things, no matter how many systems they try to adopt. This is just a story. We all use a system to manage our time, organised or not. You may just need to upgrade your system to a better one, and be disciplined enough to use it to manage your time. That is what elite leaders do.

The Energisers: Those who have a bias towards energy

The *Energisers*, it is no surprise, push hard with energy. When faced with a piece of work, their catchcry is: *'Let's do this!'* They rely less on organising systems, task lists and clean inboxes. They just get stuff done. From the outside they can seem chaotic, but there is usually a system in place—it's just in their head. Just because they rely less on structured systems does not mean they are disorganised, although sometimes they are.

Energisers are possibly more focused on outcomes than the actions that Organisers tend to focus on. When they are under pressure or stressed, rather than put a plan in place, they just want to do something that starts them on the path to achieving the outcome needed.

They love meeting with others, and although this is a bit of a generalisation, there could be a correlation between being an Energiser and an extrovert. In fact, they are prone to filling up every crack of available time in the schedule with meetings, running from one meeting to the next, pushing through with all of that unbridled energy.

They want to be in the moment, and to deal with whatever the most pressing issue or opportunity is. They are really good at bringing others on the journey, and inspiring others to get more done than they thought they were capable of. They love a deadline, but only when it is looming, and requires energy to smash it.

When I talk to Lisa about how she likes to work, she shudders with revulsion when she thinks about organising herself with lists and schedules. In fact, she took one look at one of my books and said to herself, 'I'm not bloody reading that!' I love her honesty and her energy. Now, of course, she does use a calendar, and makes lists, I am sure, but her main thing is energy, and leveraging the highly organised people around her.

People like Lisa use the tools at their disposal to keep information and their time organised, but prefer others to do this for them if possible. Senior Energisers rely on their EA or PA a lot, and will often leave the management of their schedule and inbox to them.

Energiser strengths recap:

- get a lot done when they focus on a topic

- are able to smash deadlines when needed

- tend to be across a lot of topics and issues

- pull others along with them

- seem to have endless amounts of energy.

Energisers have their challenges too. They can be a nightmare to work with, as they can be so chaotic. The people around them have to pick up the pieces, and can waste time chasing them for direction or input on work. Their inboxes are often overflowing, and they can miss emails easily. In fact, a typical Energiser behaviour with email is to respond to your email immediately or never respond at all!

They can be highly reactive, and force others to be reactive with them. They often leave things until the last minute, and tell themselves that they are tracking well when they have a deadline looming. Unfortunately, they don't recognise the negative impact that this has on those around them or on their own stress levels.

They can waste time looking for information that should have been better organised in the first place. Time can also be wasted fixing mistakes created by running at 100 miles an hour all the time. They can be challenged with technology, so get frustrated when they feel they should know more about technology, but don't.

Other people working with an Energiser can end up exhausted very quickly, trying to keep up. They set a fast pace, and forget that not everyone has the same energy levels as them. They can work long hours by choice, and end up setting an expectation (real or perceived) that others should too. Emails at 11 pm are not unusual.

Of course, their energy has a limit, so they do tend to crash and burn eventually. Weekends can be spent in a heap, and holidays are a temporary fix — that is if they take a holiday in the first place. Some don't. Some do, but are glued to their phone or laptop rather than relaxing. Of course, this has consequences for their family and significant others.

Energiser challenges recap:

- can be highly disorganised

- can feel stressed and burnt out

- exhausting for others

- things slip through the cracks and get forgotten

- time wasted on rework and looking for information

- reactive approach to work

- tend to crash and burn eventually.

If you identify with being an Energiser, be confident that you possess an ability that is hard to teach. Your abundant energy is a gift, but you need to use it wisely, and ensure that it does not create problems for you or your team down the track. When you can bolster the power of your energy with excellent time and focusing strategies, you can become unstoppable.

Because your preference might be to operate at 120 per cent energy for every activity until you finally crash, you need to think carefully about how you manage the flow. What are the times in the day or the week when you have the most energy? What activities in your week require the most energy, and where could you conserve energy in your week? And how does your penchant for energy affect those around you? Are you pulling them along in a productive way, or are you like a bull in a china shop, creating havoc wherever you go?

Tips for managing the resource of energy

Time is an external resource; energy is very much an internal resource that we need to manage. And the key is flow. Our energy ebbs and flows, and if we can control this flow, we ensure that we bring everything to the key moments in our role.

If you overuse energy as an organising resource, you risk peaking too early or burning out or both. Managing the energy flow is a subtle art—knowing when to go hard, and when to pull back. Knowing when to dial it up to high, or when to conserve energy for later.

When you plan your week, it is worth identifying the key activities or meetings that will require the highest levels of your energy. How are you going to conserve energy beforehand? How are you going to ensure you are fully prepared so that your energy can flow unhindered? How are you going to come down afterwards so you don't stay in a manic energy state all day? Having a ramp-up and ramp-down strategy can be useful here. I have a routine in the 30 minutes before I give a presentation that helps me get into the right 'state'. Reviewing my key message, listening to music, getting into my stage gear and getting my head clear for the delivery — they all play a part of getting me into the right energy state.

It is also worth thinking about your natural energy rhythms throughout the day. Many people are morning people, and have the highest amounts of energy in the first couple of hours of the day. If that is you, protect those golden hours for work that requires a higher level of energy (not emails). That is not to say you should arrange your big presentation for that time, as a meeting or a presentation will automatically elevate your energy levels. But a key priority that needs your energy is better done in a high energy timeslot in your day. Knowing when to operate in a low energy mode is useful too. In fact, this is a key learning for the Energisers amongst us.

The Analysers: Those who have a bias towards focus

The final group is probably the rarer of the three groups. The *Analysers* have a bias for getting their work done by concentrating their focus. When faced with a piece of work, their catchcry is: *'Let's think about this!'*

They have the ability to study things in detail, and go deep in their work. They yearn for space and time alone to do their work uninterrupted, and can immerse themselves in a topic or a task for hours on end. They rely less on systems to organise what they need to do, but rather deep dive into the meaty work in front of them. Because of this bias, they often choose roles that benefit from their skillset, so it is no surprise that they can often be analysts, programmers, lawyers or researchers — all are roles that benefit from deep focus.

They can also hold a lot of information in their head at once, and can zoom in and out of a problem easily, going from the abstract to the concrete as needed. They are clear about their priorities, and manage their attention to focus on these things as much as possible. Their key organising tool is their head, and they probably believe that no computer or system comes close to the power of their mind. Analysers rely less on energy to get stuff done. In fact, they probably find people with too much energy distracting, and can be challenged by them. When an Analyser is put under pressure, they might default to making some space to think about what needs to happen.

While they like to work alone much of the time, they are good working in groups, as long as the work is worthy. They can mobilise a group around a problem, and can collaborate to achieve great outcomes.

I had a discussion with a friend of mine, Alex Hagen, who identifies with being an Analyser. He is a very high-level thinker, and is good, sometimes too good, at practicing deep focus. He told me that he had tried in vain for many years to follow productivity systems to help him to manage his time. None of them worked for him. He then tried to follow his energy, but it was still not right. Over time he settled on a way of managing his focus, which gave him the control he felt he needed to be productive.

Analyser strengths recap:

- good at focusing on important work
- able to hold many things in their head
- can analyse and problem-solve well
- avoid distractions and distracting people
- acutely aware of the optimal environment for their productivity.

Analysers sometimes fail to follow organising systems for their day-to-day work, so can be a bit unresponsive to emails, and a bit scatter-brained with the day-to-day tasks. In some extreme cases, they can be like a brilliant scientist, doing amazing work, but forgetting basic things like shopping and eating.

They don't like to be distracted by anything that is not their most important focus, so can be frustrating to work with, as they drag their heels on the responses and inputs that other people need from them. They can be resentful when other people interrupt their deep focus, and hate being dragged into pointless meetings (some might say not a weakness at all). They are unresponsive to other people's urgency, but create a lot of their own as they leave things until the last minute through forgetfulness.

They can find it challenging to re-emerge from deep focus sessions, and in some cases, attach little meaning to time, which can be frustrating for others around them. Their system for organising their thoughts, if they have one, probably only makes sense to them, made up of a random scatter of sticky notes and scribbles.

Analyser challenges recap:

- can be disorganised

- can be forgetful

- frustrating to work with if needing their input

- self-sabotage by missing deadlines

- can get stuck in deep focus.

If you identify with being an Analyser, with the innate ability to focus deeply, you will be one of the few that Cal Newport, author of *Deep Work*, says can thrive in the workplace of the future. But it cannot be at the expense of managing your time or your energy, because your team needs the benefit of those if they are to thrive with you.

Tips to manage the resource of focus

Our focus is an internal resource greatly impacted by the external world, so managing our environment is critical. This can involve everything from the location you are working from, such as the office or home, to managing the surrounding noise. That could mean dampening distractions and interruptions, such as email alerts, or surrounding yourself with ambient noise to aid concentration.

When I write, I am best locked away up the coast, but of course that does not mean that I can only write in that location. When that is not possible, then I do my best to create a reasonable environment that allows for focus. For you, this could mean booking a meeting room, working from home, going to a café for an hour or putting headphones on in your open-plan office. But be organised about it and plan for your needs ahead of time.

Compressing time can also be an effective strategy when trying to carve out focus time in a busy schedule. Don't set yourself up for failure by aiming for too much unrealistic focus time, then give it away when some urgent issue comes up to derail your plans. One of my clients was frustrated that she had intended to do a planning exercise, and had put aside two hours to do it, but ended up being sidetracked, and it never got done.

My advice, given her very senior and very busy role, was that two hours was probably too much time, and it was always likely to end in failure. Next time, I said, plan 30 minutes to nail it, but stick to it. Better good and finished than great and unfinished!

Finally, have an exit strategy for focus time. Set a time limit and find a way to decompress at the end of the focus session. I often do something physical, even for five minutes, to shake it off before moving on to my more normal work. This could be a walk, some stretching exercises or a trip to get a quick coffee.

I discuss more focus strategies in chapter 3.

Which style do you identify with?

I am hesitant to label people or force people into a category, but I do think, in this case, it is useful to think about your bias. This will have implications for every other chapter in the book, and having some self-awareness around your organising style can help you make decisions about how you organise yourself and work with others.

Was there a style that resonated strongly for you? Could you, like me, see that you are a natural Organiser? Or maybe, like Lisa, big on energy? Or maybe you are a ninja at analysing. Whichever fits best for you, know that you are probably not

100 per cent any of these archetypes. But you are likely to have a bias for one and can probably identify a second as your backup preference. Have a think about how you operate and what your primary and secondary biases might be. Then go next level by learning to use all three resources as needed, depending on the work at hand or the situation.

Choose the right resource for the job at hand

The most effective leaders not only understand their bias, they develop the ability to switch from one resource to another as needed. They can move from managing their time, to managing their energy, to managing their focus. Even though they may prefer one, they can lean on the others at will, almost like a footballer who kicks with their dominant right foot, but can score a goal almost as effectively with their left.

The first step in developing the ability to switch between styles is to recognise your current reality, or which bias you lean most towards, and work on strategies to develop your abilities in using the other resources. Then work out which resource is best in which situation.

There is work that is best managed with the resource of time. A good example of this might be ensuring you respond to key emails in a timely way. Being responsive (to the appropriate emails) requires you to manage your time in a proactive way. There is work that is best served through energy, such as a critical meeting or presentation that requires all of your energy to influence the room, or a negotiation that will require you to be 100 per cent engaged in what is happening. And there is work that requires deep focus, maybe absorbing a piece of analysis to inform a key decision, or writing a detailed report or proposal.

There is a time and a place for each, and your ability to turn on each is a next-level ability.

A leader also needs to understand how to carefully manage each of these resources, and to use them at the right moment. I once saw Counting Crows, one of my favourite bands, do a sound check in the afternoon before their show. The lead singer, Adam Duritz, sang about four songs, but was quite reserved and quiet, not talking very much to the small crowd who had been invited. The drummer told a few jokes, but Adam seemed almost shy and stand-offish.

That night, as they performed the actual show, he was a different person — energised, vocal, fun, a real showman. It became obvious to me that he had been managing his energy in the afternoon, making sure he kept his reserves of energy contained until the show itself.

I use a similar strategy myself with training. During COVID, when all of our training went online, and tended to be broken down into smaller webinars rather than full-day training sessions, I ended up sometimes running two or three two-hour webinars in a day. That could be six hours of delivery in a day, which in the old face-to-face format, was pretty normal. But I found my energy getting too diluted when I ran multiple sessions in a day. I was not able to deliver at 100 per cent by session two or three, so I made a decision. I now only run one session a day, and I manage my energy to bring 100 per cent of my energy to that session.

● ● ●

I guess, to round off this topic, that using these three resources effectively comes down to balance, or the ability to use these resources in balance. But this is not the only balance a leader needs to think about. The next chapter will explore balance in detail.

Reflections and intentions

- Take some time to understand your primary bias: are you an Organiser, an Energiser or an Analyser?

- What would your secondary bias be?

- What insights does this give you about how you manage your work?

- What insights does it give you about how you work with your team?

- Thinking about the activities that your role requires, which of these are best managed with time? Which need more energy? Which are best served with focus?

CHAPTER 2
Find your balance

Every Monday morning, I partake in one-on-one training with a fantastic, but very uncompromising, personal trainer called Adrienne. I am not very good at maintaining discipline around things like regular exercise, so she is my intentionality strategy for fitness. Every Monday I know I have to go through some pain to set me up for the rest of the week, and for the rest of my life.

Every now and again, when she wants to work on my core strength, she gets me up on one leg on a balancing ball. I have to stand on a semi-circular inflatable ball on one leg for as long as possible without falling. I am terrible at this, and fall over quite quickly and regularly.

As I stand there, arms and legs flailing to try to stay balanced, Adrienne will often remind me that balance comes from the core. She will get me to engage my abdominal muscles, and focus on those. Soon enough, things usually settle down and I manage to stay balanced in a much more controlled and harmonious way.

Staying balanced in a work context is similar. My flailing arms and legs in this instance are a good analogy for the busy activity we often throw at the problem when we experience a lack of balance. We think that more activity will help us to get more done, and in turn, allow us to create some balance moving forward. But of course, it rarely does. We just end up taking on more and more, and we fill whatever space we have with more activity. And so the cycle goes.

We need to build core strength to achieve balance. In this case, not abdominal strength, but a strong mindset that can remain focused on what is important, but remain flexible enough to change when necessary. This takes work, practice and, most of all, conviction.

There is much talk these days about work/life balance, and many organisations have begun to put skills training and development strategies in place to help their people achieve better balance. Unfortunately, often these organisations talk the talk, but don't walk the walk when it comes to creating a culture that will support true work/life balance. They talk about it, but they place demands on their people that can only be met by compromising work/life balance. Many managers and leaders end up working long hours to get everything done. We may now have more flexible working arrangements as a result of the shift to hybrid working after the COVID pandemic, but many people still feel the need to work a long day, have dinner and then get the laptop out after dinner or after the kids are in bed.

It's common practice for leaders to work some of the weekend, and for many to send and receive emails after hours. This lack of balance puts a lot of pressure on the leaders, and over time, leads to increased stress, fatigue and risk of burnout.

We need to reframe the idea that working long hours is part of being a senior leader.

One consulting firm that I worked with in 2022 identified fatigue and burnout as the number-one risk to their business, globally.

In some ways, I feel that creating a working environment that will allow us to get what we need to get done in a reasonable number of hours cannot only be the responsibility of the organisation. Of course, the organisation has a huge responsibility here, but each of us, individually, has to play a role in creating a work style that leads to work/life balance as well — especially leaders, who are the example that others follow.

We need to reframe the idea that working long hours is part of being a senior leader. This may be true, but only up to a certain point. I think it is more useful to recognise that this is a mindset that has just become the norm in the modern workplace. My father was a senior leader in a semi-government body in Dublin in the 1970s. Although he was a divisional director leading a large team, he did not work particularly long hours. He was in the office by 9 am, home by 5.30 pm and always took a lunch break in the canteen. Was he ineffective as a leader working these hours? No, of course not. That was the environment that he worked in as a leader, and that was his norm. Can we go back to those halcyon days? Probably not. But I believe we need to move back in that direction.

When I talk about balance, I like to focus less on work/life balance, and more on what I call work/work balance. There are lots of activities that consume our time, energy and focus during our workday. If we don't get the balance right with these activities, then we tend to throw our work/life balance out of whack, a bit like if we don't align our posture correctly, we can throw our spine out of whack. And once that happens, we are in a world of pain. And, of course, thinking back to my workouts with Adrienne, if we can build a core strength around balance, we are less likely to get out of alignment.

Work/work balance

The secret to achieving balance and managing everything that needs to be done, whilst maintaining your sanity and having a life, is to achieve three key balances within your role. They are the balance between:

- time in *meetings* and time protected for *priorities*

- *reactive* work and *proactive* work

- a focus on *inputs* and a focus on *outcomes.*

I have this image in my mind of these words balancing on either end of a seesaw. When the seesaw is level, all is good — we are in balance. If the seesaw is tipped all the way up on one side, it could signify an imbalance. All too often, if there is an imbalance, it is usually heavily weighted to one end of the seesaw. With the pairings above, I typically see meetings, reactive work and focus on inputs on the lower side of the seesaw, as these are the activities that we stack too high. It is not a coincidence that these imbalances are primarily driven by others. Being proactive, protecting time for priorities and working on outcomes is work that is driven by us (see figure 2.1, overleaf). The seesaws don't always need to be in the middle, perfectly balanced, but if there is a pattern of imbalance, this can be problematic.

Let us look at each in turn, and examine why each can get out of balance, and what you can do about it.

Balance 1: Meetings versus priorities

If I had to choose a dominant productivity issue senior managers and leaders face, I would have to say it is a lack of balance between time in meetings and time protected for other work. And this is especially true for leaders who have an

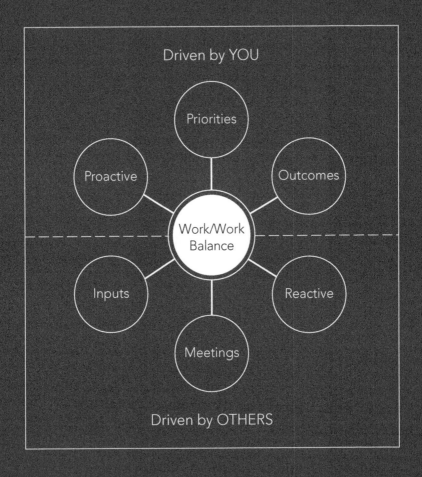

Figure 2.1: Work/work balance

energy bias, and preference meeting with others over working by themselves a lot of the time.

As a leader, we need to fit several different types of activities into our week. We need time to:

- meet with others

- work on priorities

- be responsive to communications

- think

- have more informal conversations with stakeholders and teams

- plan and prepare.

Now, I do not want to get rid of meetings; they are not the bad guy here. Meetings are a common, legitimate and, I daresay, essential way to get work done in any organisation. But if you think about it, they are a bit of a clunky, cumbersome tool. They can take longer than needed, they can involve too many people, they can be poorly organised or even downright aimless. They can waste so much group time if not organised and managed really well.

In a smaller team or organisation, time in meetings is usually reasonably contained. In my business, whilst I do attend a number of meetings and client engagements each week, I enjoy a healthy balance between my time in meetings and time available for the rest of my work. I am lucky, because my team is small, and I have limited pressure on my schedule, and also a high level of control over how my schedule is run. But what I tend to see in larger teams, and especially in large corporates and multinationals, is leaders feeling they don't have as much control over the demands on their time purely because of the size of the team, the complexity of the work and the interaction between their role and the rest of the organisation.

While time in meetings, especially at the senior level, may be unavoidable, our schedules should not be so overloaded that we have no time to get anything else done. We need time in our week to get to our other priorities. These activities cannot be relegated to after hours if we expect to maintain some form of work/life balance. And this is what happens so much of the time: We give most of our time away to meetings, and do not protect enough time for our other work during core working hours.

To get more balance in your schedule, you need to spend less time in meetings. There is no other way around this. Now you may be thinking at this point, 'I am a senior executive, and the more senior I become, the more meetings I am expected to have.' Many executives I speak to hold this view, and it certainly is the norm in a lot of organisations. I have seen very senior people cram 15 or more meetings into a day and think nothing of it.

Call me crazy, but I actually think that the more senior you become, the fewer meetings you should attend! Here is my logic. When we start our career as a junior worker (and of course this is role dependant) our meeting workload is probably quite low. We might be invited to a few meetings each week to gain experience, but most of our time is spent doing stuff rather than discussing stuff, or deciding things. As we work our way into more senior roles, especially those that involve managing people, we take on a greater and greater meeting workload.

As we reach senior-level management (or middle-level in a large organisation), we can expect our schedule to be bursting at the seams with meetings. And so it continues until we retire (or burn out). The dotted line in figure 2.2 (overleaf) plots the typical meeting workload as we progress from junior to senior.

I believe that every leader should hit a point where they make a significant shift in thinking and operating rhythm, and they actively work on strategies to reduce their time in meetings, allowing themselves the space to think, to be available to their team, and concentrate their focus on proactive and strategic actions and horizons.

We have said that time, as with energy and focus, is a finite resource, and there is always an opportunity cost. Every time you say 'yes' to something, you are also saying 'no' to something else! If you are saying 'yes' to too many meetings, what is the opportunity cost if you look at the use of your time more holistically. When are you going to do the other types of activities that your role demands if you are always in meetings?

I was asked to do some work with a senior leadership team from a large bank in Australia in 2020. I remember it was my first live face-to-face session since the COVID outbreak had locked everything down. I had about 12 senior leaders in the room, each responsible for over 100 people in their teams. Balance came up as an issue, so I decided to do a bit of an experiment (see figure 2.3 on page 46).

I drew a chart on the whiteboard that allowed them to roughly identify how much of their core working hours, in percentage terms, they spent in meetings versus time protected for other work during the week. One by one I had them come to the front of the room and draw a line on the chart where they felt their current reality was at. Did they feel they had an even 50/50 split between time in meetings versus time spent on other work? Was it 60/40? Was it 70/30? One by one they drew their line, and low and behold, 11 out of 12 of them felt it was a 90/10

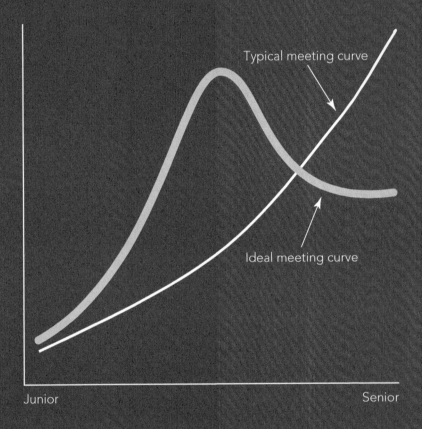

Figure 2.2: The meeting workload curve

split! That is 90 per cent of their time spent in meetings by the way, not the other way around. Their seesaw was way out of balance!

This was a sobering moment for the team. Of course, as senior managers, they knew a lot of their time was spent in meetings, but I don't think any of them had thought it was such an uneven balance. One member of the team put his line at the 70/30 mark. This intrigued me, so I asked him what made him different to the rest of the group. He informed me with a grin that he had only been a part of the team for two weeks, and nobody knew he existed yet! I am sure that has changed for him by now, unfortunately.

So, there was a realisation that way too much of their time was being spent in meetings. We discussed the impact of this, and they all agreed that they tended to allow their schedule to fill up with meetings from 8 am onwards, and usually finished their last meeting at about 6 pm. This meant that the next couple of hours were usually spent catching up on emails, and after they got home and had dinner, they got the laptop out to do another hour or two of 'real work'. Work/life balance? I think not.

So, I next asked them to come back up to the whiteboard and draw a line at the ideal balance point. If they could wave a magic wand and change the status quo, where would they put the line? This time, some of the answers varied. Some felt that they would like a 50/50 split, but felt that 60/40 was more realistic. Others felt they would be happy with 70/30. Either way, a massive improvement compared to 90/10 in my view.

Why not give this exercise a go yourself? Grab a pen and draw a line on figure 2.3 (overleaf) where you feel your current reality is. Then draw an aspirational line where you would like the balance to sit. How much of a gap is there? What are you going to do about it?

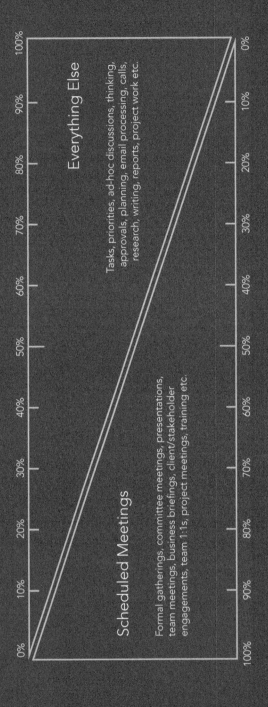

Figure 2.3: Time spent in meetings vs time spent on everything else

The leadership team that I worked with on this exercise aspired to make a shift, but the question I posed to them was: What were they going to do differently to achieve it? How were they going to protect their schedules, especially when they were working in a culture that was very meeting heavy, where others put enormous pressure on their schedules every day?

So, we rolled up our sleeves and got to work, brainstorming practical strategies that they could employ individually and as a team to create some work/work balance.

Don't be a victim of your schedule — own it! If you don't own it, other people will happily own it for you, and they don't care about your work/work balance as much as you do yourself.

It always makes me chuckle when leaders who I work with complain to me about how full their schedule is. When I ask, 'Whose fault is that?' there is often a lot of finger-pointing at the organisation, their boss, their team, the marketing department, IT and, of course, clients. But the reality is usually that the finger should be turned around and pointed back at the executive themselves. They were the ones who accepted the meeting requests in the first place, or allowed their EA to make poor judgements on their behalf.

When you stop being a victim in a culture of busyness, you'll be surprised how much agency you actually have. Think about a leader that you have worked under in your career who was really on top of their time management and prioritisation. They were probably taking a lot of responsibility over the schedule to the point of ruthlessness. The best leaders do. This is the type of next-level lift that I talked about at the start of this section.

What practical strategies can you bring to create more balance between time in meetings and time working on priorities? Look back for a start!

Look back: Hindsight could save you time

The first thing you can do is to learn from your past and make choices about your future. In a recent coaching call with a client, we explored the split between their time in meetings and time protected for other work. As usual, it was out of whack. We discussed creating some balance in their schedule, and she was keen to aim for a 70/30 split.

Although she was keen to protect more time, and had made a decision about her ideal split, she had a challenge. Looking at her calendar for the coming month, she had no space left to protect. Her schedule was already full. When I suggested cancelling or declining some of those meetings, she said she could lose a few, but she felt compelled to attend most. I felt she was not being ruthless enough, so I tried something a bit different.

I asked her to review all the meetings that she attended over the *last* month. With meeting quality and outcomes in mind, I asked her to identify any meetings that:

- should not have gone ahead because they did not achieve a worthwhile outcome or could have been dealt with in another way

- she should not have attended because they were not a good use of her time, or she was the wrong person to be in that meeting

- could have been shortened as they were poorly organised and unfocused, or just had too much time allocated to begin with.

She printed her calendar for the previous month, and lo and behold, identified many hours that she could have freed up.

Unfortunately, that boat had sailed, but when she looked forward at the coming month again, I could see a more ruthless glint in her eye. I left her to make some decisions about which meetings she should cancel, decline, delegate or shorten. If she could not do any of those things, hopefully she at least took measures to ensure the meetings she attended were well organised and focused.

I believe this is one of the most powerful things you can do to create more balance in your schedule. And don't just do it once, do it at least quarterly! And don't just do it for yourself—I have seen CEOs do this at an organisational level, reviewing regular meetings across the organisation and culling what was deemed unnecessary, or no longer necessary.

Balance 2: Reactive versus proactive

A funny thing happens in organisations. There is often a push to have workers, especially leaders, working on the things that are most important. Yet the organisation conspires against that ideal, and forces people to work reactively rather than proactively. Our over-sensitivity to urgency can keep us stuck in the operational weeds too much of the time. Everyone is extremely busy, but it can sometimes feel like we are not getting anywhere because we are reacting so much to the daily issues that crop up.

I write about urgency in detail in my book *Urgent!*, and it has become a passion project for me to help teams and organisations work less reactively and more proactively. We all have urgent stuff that demands our instant focus, but when reactivity becomes our default way of working, or becomes the default way that others work with us, it causes massive problems.

Reactivity:

- causes increased stress and tension

- distracts us from what is really important

- disrupts our plans and priorities

- leads to mistakes and rework

- is often caused by someone (possibly yourself) not managing their work in a timely way.

When we spend time on proactive work, we make life better for ourselves and others. We tend to work in a more measured way, improving the quality of our thinking and the outputs we produce. We get ahead of the curve and proactively move more of the right work forward. And we reduce the risk of additional work having to be done at the last minute because we are already on top of it. We anticipate more issues, and put contingency plans in place to minimise them.

Of course, we can't work exclusively on proactive work, as the demands of any business require us to be responsive to day-to-day needs. It requires us to clearly appreciate the difference between responsiveness and being reactive. Many of us believe we are being responsive, when we are actually reacting without taking a moment to understand what is happening and what is needed. There is a subtle but important difference between reactivity and responsiveness.

Leaders who have a bias for energy can be very challenged by this. If they rely on their energy to get them through work and deadlines, they can leave too many things to the last minute, creating a situation where they have to put out fires, but these are, unfortunately, fires they have lit themselves. If you have a bias for focus, this can also be a problem for you, as you immerse yourself in deep work, leaving other work until the last minute or until others are chasing you.

Always question urgency

I remember a Wham! video in the 1980s where George Michael is wearing a T-shirt with *'Choose Life'* emblazoned on it. I want a T-shirt with *'Choose Proactivity'* on it! Reactivity is a choice. If you allow urgency to rule in your team, and you manage your own work in a last-minute way, you are choosing reactivity.

Many people see urgency as an outside force that they have no control over. But this is rarely true. There are always things that need your urgent attention, but if you look at these things closely, you might find that some of them were never actually urgent at all. Or you might find that they were urgent, but the urgency could have been avoided if you, or someone else, managed the work proactively.

I often hear parents talking about how messy their teenage child's room is. Often these teenagers try to keep their room tidy, but it defeats them. They can adopt a victim mentality, claiming it is just too hard, as if they have no control in the situation. But their messy room comes from a series of choices they have made, and had control over. Every pile of dirty clothes on the floor, and dirty plate on their study desk was a choice they made.

We also make our own choices when it comes to managing our work, yet we often feel that the urgency and reactivity is external to us and out of our control. But we can take control by choosing to work proactively. We can choose to manage our own work in a more proactive way by scheduling time in our calendar or a task in a task list. We can also choose to never allow urgency to pass us by without questioning it. *Is this truly urgent? Why is it urgent? What could we do differently next time? What was the opportunity cost to the team?*

Questions like this, consistently asked by leaders, create more proactive cultures. You can make a huge difference for yourself and your team by doing this. And you can create more balance in your week by dialling down the urgency just a bit.

Balance 3: Inputs versus outcomes

I am sure this imbalance must be the bane of many a senior leader. You look ahead at each coming year with aspirations of shifting the dial on many strategic initiatives, yet often seem to get dragged right into the day-to-day operational issues and dramas that need your attention but take you away from the strategic. If you are not careful, you find yourself spending the day swatting these issues away rather than doing the work that truly has an impact. You end up working on inputs rather than outcomes.

You may not feel you can ignore the issues that come up, and nor should you. But you should create a more balanced approach to your work so that you are moving both inputs and outcomes forward in an even way.

It's probably not true to say that you don't get to the outcomes and the more strategic work, because you could not survive for long in a leader's role if you didn't. But it always seems hard, doesn't it? Creating a balance between the inputs and the outcomes requires a clear focus, and a ruthless approach to how you spend your time. It requires conviction in your priorities, and a mindset that questions every action, and the opportunity cost of every action.

Ronald Heifetz and Marty Linsky talk about what they call 'The Balcony' in their book *Leadership On the Line*. It is a well-known metaphor they created to describe a leader's need to get out of the fray of 'doing', or as they describe it, off the dance floor and onto the balcony where they can get some perspective.

This allows them to see patterns they might miss when they're in the middle of the action. A leader cannot always stay on the balcony, as they cannot affect what is happening from up there, but they need the skill of moving their perspective to that position on a regular basis.

The context in which the authors use this metaphor is when thinking about complex problems, but I think it holds true for a leader's activity in their day or week. You need to spend time in the thick of the action, on the dance floor, being responsive to the needs of your team and the organisation, but you also you need to step up onto the balcony to get some perspective and to work on the strategic. There needs to be a balance, and your time, energy and focus should operate at both levels.

Make time to plan

For me, spending more time on outcomes comes down to personal planning. Now, I know that, as a leader, you are involved in a lot of planning. But this often happens at the organisational level, the team level or the project level. What we sometimes forget is to plan at the personal level. When this final layer of planning is missing, it creates a gap between what we are trying to achieve and what we are actually spending our time on.

In *Smart Work*, I discussed the concept of centralising all of your actions (meetings and priorities) into one organising tool, such as Microsoft Outlook. I suggested creating a workflow across your week and future weeks, where you can see your scheduled commitments in your calendar, and your priorities and tasks for each day in your task list. I will talk more about this concept in chapter 3.

This centralised system for managing actions could be a repository for two sets of actions that arrive from different places. It can be filled by *inputs* from other people, such as meeting invites, meeting actions and emails, which are all things you need to be responsive to. But it should also be filled with your *outcomes* in mind, with the next-step actions that you can proactively drive into your own schedule or task list (see figure 2.4).

Stephen Covey talks to this concept in his book *First Things First*, using the analogy of rocks and sand. He said to schedule the rocks in first, the rocks being the important and probably more strategic things you should be working on. If you get them into your schedule first, the other, more operational sand can fit in the space around the rocks. It's an old but still relevant analogy, and many leaders I have worked with have come across the concept on their journey, and yet they still don't do it consistently!

I recommend building a routine around weekly planning. This should not have the one-dimensional focus of just looking at your schedule for the next week and working out what you need to prepare for or do. It should also involve looking back over the previous week to tie off any loose ends, then organise the next week, and even look a few weeks ahead to anticipate what is coming. But, finally, it should include some time spent looking at the big picture, thinking about the strategic work in your role, and scheduling any next-step actions into your calendar or task list for the coming weeks.

I believe that, as leaders, we do not allow ourselves enough time to simply think. We almost feel ashamed of being busy inside our head but not busy with our mouth or body. A solid weekly planning routine creates space to think!

I wonder if we, as senior managers, feel a bit of guilt about taking time out to think, to reflect, to problem-solve? Most leaders would value more time during core working hours to think and reflect. They rarely get this golden time in their week, and instead resign themselves to doing their thinking in their own time. This, of

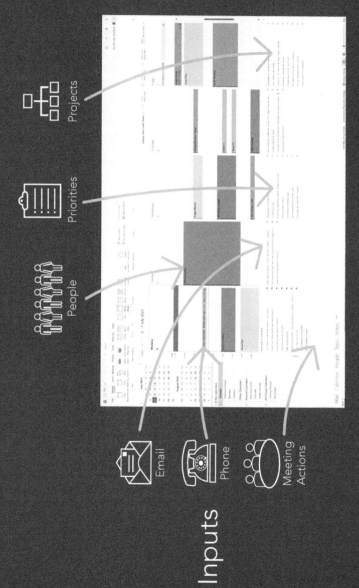

Outcomes

People   Priorities   Projects

Email   Phone   Meeting Actions

Inputs

Figure 2.4: Fill your calendar with both inputs and outcomes

course, has implications for work/life balance. Leaders need time to switch off, to recharge and to refresh just like everyone else. Leaders often have loved ones or families who not only crave their presence and time, but their full attention as well.

I always ask senior people who I work with: 'Do you feel you get enough time to think?' Invariably the answer is 'no'. But you should make time for thinking, as this is what you get paid to do. This is where a lot of your value lies. You can't make good decisions, solve complex problems or develop new ideas when you are moving at 100 miles an hour, in back-to-back meetings and working within a highly compressed schedule.

Leaders who have a bias for focus may find this pairing a bit more balanced, as their mind is more geared towards thinking and reflection. They cherish time for a deep dive on a strategy, issue or plan. Time and energy lovers may struggle.

● ● ●

So, we have explored the balance between meetings and priorities, between the proactive and the reactive, and between inputs and outcomes. If you work on these balances, you will find it easier to achieve an overall balance between work and life.

Reflections and intentions

- Which of the three balances is most unbalanced for you?

- Where are you feeling most balanced?

- If you were to work on rebalancing one of these areas, which would it be?

- Think about your preferred productivity style (Organiser, Energiser, Analyser). How does your productivity style impact your balance?

CHAPTER 3

Develop deep and wide focus

In his book *Deep Work*, Cal Newport suggests that the ability to perform what he calls 'deep work', or the ability to focus deeply on a topic, is becoming increasingly rare at the same time as it is becoming increasingly more valuable in our economy. This skill that can set us apart in a crowded workplace, one possibly changed immeasurably by AI and other technologies in the future, is harder to practice as our workplaces become more distracting, and our workdays become busier and more compressed.

For leaders, being able to focus deeply is one of the skills that we must practice and protect if we are going to truly add value in our role. But it is not just about being able to focus deeply. The real skill for leaders is being able to focus deep and wide, and to move between these states with ease (see figure 3.1, overleaf).

As we have already discussed, being productive is a mix of managing your time, energy and focus. When it comes to focus, how we manage our attention, and subsequently, how we then manage our time and energy around the things we need to do,

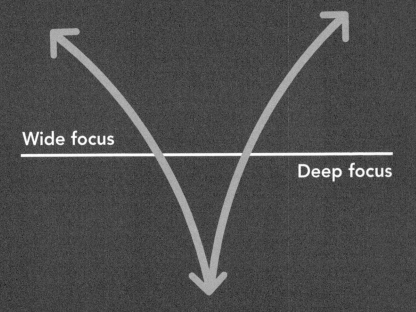

Concentrating widely on multiple topics

Wide focus

Deep focus

Concentrating deeply on one topic

Figure 3.1: Deep and wide focus

is key. An effective leader needs to be able to focus in two ways. They need to be able to:

- divide their focus across a wide range of topics or issues, ensuring nothing slips through the cracks

- concentrate deeply on certain topics in order to understand concepts or issues, which increases their ability to problem-solve, give direction or make decisions.

This is a challenging dynamic for many, but I have seen some leaders do this really well. Much like rubbing their stomach and patting their head at the same time (a challenge I attempted unsuccessfully many times as a child), effective leaders seem to be able to focus on many things at once, whilst at the same time being able to zoom into fine detail on certain issues or topics.

I recently read a story about Elon Musk at the launch of his first rocket, *Falcon One*. After years of blood, sweat and tears, he and his team were in the final ten-minute countdown to the first launch. You can imagine that he was focused on many things that were happening in the room and out on the launchpad. But at this moment he also chose to badger the flight director about a design detail for one of their future rockets.

Understandably, the flight director was incredulous that he was interrupted about such a detail at this critical point in time, but this is just the nature of Elon Musk's brain. He is able to both zoom in on a detail about a future project while zooming out to focus on the many things happening at the launch. He could hold both of those perspectives in his head at the same time. I call this deep and wide focus. They require different skillsets, and different external supports to manage them effectively.

Deep focus is like a balancing act in a circus, where the acrobat balances a chair on their forehead, slowly moving back and forth to keep the chair from falling. It requires stillness and intense concentration. In the context of our work, deep focus also requires stillness and concentration. Stillness in the context of our environment and mind, free from distractions, and concentration in the sense of being able to focus all of your mental energy on the chosen topic to achieve a desired result.

Wide focus is more like the acrobat juggling lots of balls in the air, effortlessly throwing and catching them, never dropping any. This requires technique, quick reflexes and agility. While I could suggest that you work on expanding your brainpower and memory to manage lots of information at once, there is an easier solution.

Wide focus in our work requires a system, because our brain was never really wired to manage so many thoughts all at once. Our brain is more akin to a hard drive storing information than a CPU processing information. This part of the brain still operates as it did when we were cave men and women, dealing with simple tasks, limited inputs and stimulus, and simple needs like eating, hunting and surviving attacks from wild animals.

When managing multiple issues, opportunities, projects, people and actions, our brain cannot remember everything that it needs to, and it's especially challenging to remember things exactly *when* we need to. This is why we so often end up working reactively, because we are trying to juggle multiple balls at once with no system in place to help us. But, if we have a system that augments our ability to manage multiple things, and we consistently use this system to make our work more visible and manageable to us, our ability to move from one thing to another increases. Even at speed. This is similar to the reflexes and agility that a good juggler possesses.

Highly productive leaders are able to zoom in and zoom out, moving between wide focus to deep focus quickly.

Deep focus is hard. So is wide focus. What is even more challenging is to do both of these things at once, moving seamlessly between deep and wide focus as you go through your day or your week. Now, the reality is that you are not really doing both at exactly the same time, you're moving from one state to another quickly. Multitasking is a myth, and the reality is that those who are credited with being able to multitask are actually able to switch between tasks or contexts quickly; they don't really do multiple things at once. Highly productive leaders are able to zoom in and zoom out, moving between wide focus to deep focus quickly.

Wide focus strategies

Every senior leader I have ever worked with has a system in place to manage meetings. It's called a calendar. It may be a paper diary, but is much more likely to be an electronic calendar in MS Outlook or Google Calendar. A calendar is a system for remembering the many meetings you have scheduled over the weeks and months ahead. I think most of us would struggle if we had to keep all of our meetings in our head and remember to go to them all at the right time. We are all very comfortable with, and grateful for, this highly effective tool in our working lives.

Yet, when it comes to all the other stuff we need to remember in our role, our tasks and priorities, things we need to discuss with others, work that is due back to us, emails we need to respond to, meeting agenda items — these are often managed in a less-than-effective system. In fact, I would suggest they are managed in many different ineffective systems! Most of us tend to park these activities in lots of different places, like our inbox, notepads, sticky notes, piles of paper and, of course, our heads. No wonder we end up working reactively, trying desperately to juggle everything, but letting things slip through the cracks—or like our acrobat friend, dropping the ball altogether. We need a system to manage all of this detail, not just our meeting workload.

I believe we need an effective list that complements our effective calendar. A calendar is a tool that is perfectly fit for purpose when it comes to managing meetings. Likewise, we need a tool that is perfectly fit for purpose when it comes to managing our priorities. Some sort of a list might be the answer.

The question is what type of list? There are many types of lists that go from simple to complex. A checklist is a simple list that ensures completeness and thoroughness. Pilots use checklists before they take off to ensure everything that needs to be checked has been checked. In that context, it is the perfect tool, but it is probably a bit too simplistic for managing multiple priorities in between a heavy meeting schedule.

A project plan could be described as a more complex list, with a list of the project tasks, their start and due dates, and even dependency links between each activity. But maybe this is too complex for our needs here. We need a happy medium that is fit for purpose for day to day work.

I have always been a devotee of using a 'dated list' in MS Outlook to manage day-to-day priorities and activities. This is because, in my busy week, time is very limited, and my schedule reasonably full, so I want to be clear about what I need to do each day, and realistic about what I can get done. This promotes a balanced and proactive approach to workload management. I talk about this approach in detail in *Smart Work*.

A dated list is a task list that has been divided into a series of daily lists. So rather than having one large checklist, you may have several tasks scheduled for today, a few tasks scheduled for tomorrow, and some scheduled for Friday and so on. You could either use your calendar for this, a dated task list in MS Outlook or Gmail, or a combination of both. This method of managing your priorities is most useful when time is of the essence (and let's face it, in our modern workplaces, it usually is). The benefit of scheduling your tasks for specific days is that it reduces procrastination and promotes working proactively. As a leader, you are inherently time-poor, so managing all of your work with time in mind makes sense. You will also find that your list is less overwhelming when it is broken down into more manageable chunks (see figure 3.2).

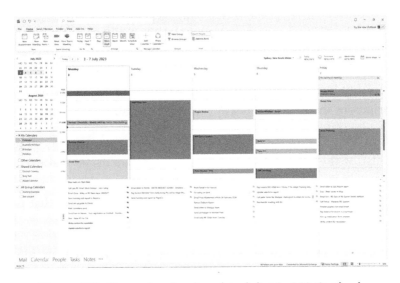

Figure 3.2: Example of a dated task list in MS Outlook

The trick to leveraging a system like this successfully is to commit fully, and use it to capture everything that you need to do. Don't fall into the trap of thinking that things are too small to capture in your list. Put everything you need to do into this one central tool.

One of my coaching clients from many years ago was a regional MD of a US bank. After several coaching sessions, I asked him what he was finding most useful and beneficial. He thought about this and replied, 'The simple act of getting things out of my head and into a tool that I trust. This frees up my mind to focus on strategy, vision and leadership.'

It is not just action items we need to juggle in our leadership roles. We also have reams and reams of information to process, store and possibly recall at the right moment. I use the word 'reams', but of course, most of this information is not contained in reams of paper, but digitally on our PC, on servers or in the cloud. It is fantastic that we can store so much information, but a massive problem presents itself in having too much information. We simply cannot access the information we need when we need it. And the quality of our work and our decision-making can depend on that information.

Again, we need a system for managing this. Not a list this time, but a place where we can capture and store the information in a way that allows for rapid retrieval when we need it.

I use a few cooking analogies in this book, I know. I watch way too many cooking shows. Bear with me, though. Top chefs, when they design their kitchens, always try to ensure that the tools they use most are within arm's reach of the work benches and stoves. They don't have time to go searching for the tools they use all the time when they are flambéing a Dover sole, so these tools tend to be hanging close by, or in cupboards next to the cooking area.

This should be true of the information we need for our work. We don't have time to search through thousands of emails or go rooting around 17 levels of filing directories to find a report that is needed for the leadership team presentation or the client briefing that afternoon. And in our senior roles, we have so many meetings, it can be hard to recall what was discussed in the last meeting, let alone the one we had three months ago.

Yet this information is the grist in the mill of a leader's work. If we want to be elite in the way we focus widely on topics and issues, we need an elite system for managing this information. And a spiral notepad won't cut it anymore. Not even a Moleskine will! Notepads are fine for some things, but they are not always the most effective tools, purely because when we capture information in them, we need to rely on a manual process to access that information. We have to rely on our brains to remember which notebook the information might be in, and we have to rely on our ability to flick from page to page to find it.

Like our action management system, our information management should be electronic in this day and age. And it should be closely tied into the different ways that information comes to us. It should be linked to how we capture meeting notes, our email, the internet and, if you are using collaborative tools like Microsoft Teams, it should ideally also be linked to this.

It should allow the easy capture of information, the ability to organise that information logically, and the means to access the information in an instant.

Oh, to have such a powerful tool! What bliss that would be! But, of course, you do have such a tool. If you are working in an organisation that uses the Microsoft Office platform, you have MS OneNote. If you are more tied to Gmail and Google tools, you can use a tool like EverNote to augment your information management abilities. I use OneNote as a core part of my organising toolkit, and apply the following strategies to manage information.

Meeting notes

I am not a massive meeting note-taker. I know that many people take detailed notes in meetings, sometimes to capture exactly what was said and agreed, sometimes as a way of understanding and synthesising the information. I work better in a meeting by listening intently and engaging eye contact with those I am meeting with, which can make it hard for me to take notes, especially electronically.

I prefer the ritual of protecting a few minutes after each meeting to download the key points, ideas or actions from the meeting in OneNote so that I can refer back to them later if required. This is invaluable if I have to produce a proposal for the client, and might be doing that a few days after we have met. My ability to quickly search for the meeting notes in OneNote provides total recall, and it only takes a couple of minutes to capture the notes after the meeting. Now, if you can capture these notes as you go in the meeting, even better.

Project information

The projects and longer-term work I deal with also lend themselves to a system for organising information, and to having it close at hand when needed. I will open a new notebook in OneNote for larger projects, or create a section in a project's notebook for smaller ones. As key information relating to the project comes into my world, I add that to my project notebook.

For example, writing this book is a project for me. One of my team members might email me some interesting research related to a topic in the book, and I want to capture that for later reference (I started collating research on this book two years before I started writing it). In Outlook, I was able to press the 'Send to OneNote' button in my inbox, and have the email and its attachments instantly copied to a page in the relevant notebook. Powerful!

Or I might be doing my own research and come across an article on the internet that is useful. One of the printers on your computer will be OneNote, so you can print webpages to OneNote. Once this information is copied to OneNote, it is instantly searchable — and I can access it through my laptop, my phone and my iPad.

People sometimes mistake my ability to recall information with being extremely clever or having a photographic memory. I am clever, but not that clever. I just use systems that allow me to focus widely on the issues and topics that require my attention. It is a bit of an unfair advantage, but we need every advantage we can get if we want to be elite.

This unfair advantage does require some discipline though: the discipline to capture the things you need to do and the information you need to refer to consistently. If we focus on this discipline, the rest will look after itself.

Many years ago, I went to a conference run by Tony Buzan, the British author who created the concept of mind mapping as a way of managing complex information. He used juggling as a theme for the conference, and everyone was given a set of three juggling sacks, which he got us using to create specific learning points.

One of these was about what we need to focus on if we want to juggle successfully. He asked the whole audience to stand up and start juggling — with no tuition. Imagine hundreds of us in a big room, all throwing and dropping these juggling sacks. He then shared the secret to successful juggling with us. Instead of focusing on catching the sacks, which is what most people do, he said to focus on throwing them. He said that if we can learn to throw in a measured, even way, the catching will look after itself. And he was right.

This is true for wide focus and the juggling of the many priorities and bits of information that make up our world. Focus on capturing the information in your system consistently, and your ability to access and recall that information at the right time will look after itself.

Daily planning

The single most powerful thing you can do to achieve focus in your day is to put an intentional plan in place each morning. Your daily plan should be focused, balanced and realistic. Focus is achieved in your plan by creating a clear view of your meetings and your priorities. Focus is more finely honed when you prioritise your task list so you are clear about what is critical to complete versus nice to complete. Your plan should have a sense of balance between your time in meetings versus time protected for priorities, which in turn leads to a realistic plan of action that gives you some hope of executing successfully.

I teach leaders to start each day by doing what I call a daily PASS.

- **P**review what you have on your plate, including both meetings and tasks in your task list.

- **A**dd whatever else you need to do.

- Then **S**ubtract anything from your schedule or task list that is unachievable or just not a priority.

- Finally, **S**equence your task list from most important to least important.

This is a simple routine that can be done first thing each morning. It takes about ten minutes, and it sets you up for success for the next ten hours. It's a no-brainer.

You may not get everything in your plan done each day, but you will run your day in a much more intentional way, and you will find it easier to maintain focus through the day.

This is a much more focused way of working for any leader, as it puts you in the driver's seat. If you want to take that focus to another level again, think about following the advice of Donna McGeorge in her book, *The First 2 Hours*. She suggests that most people do their best work in the morning rather than later in the day, so she recommends protecting the first two 'golden hours' in your day for your most important work.

I don't tend to schedule meetings before 10 am, and between 8 am and 10 am will devote some time to processing emails, planning my day using the PASS process, and getting my top three priorities done. All before my first meeting of the day! Imagine how impactful you could be if you consistently did that.

Deep focus strategies

I referenced Cal Newport and his book *Deep Work* earlier in this chapter. His hypothesis that deep work is rare and valuable in today's workplace was insightful to me as a leader. This is because my aim as a leader is to have the maximum impact that I can have in my role, for myself and my team. I realise that my role is different to yours, and that I get paid to think, and to create and to deliver content on productivity. You may feel your role contains fewer deep-focus activities and more collaborative activities, such as meeting with others, making decisions, and guiding and motivating people.

But I passionately believe that if you are a leader, the quality of what you do can only increase if you protect some of your time, energy and focus for deep focus. This is time to think, to deliberate, to understand, to problem-solve and, in many ways, to be creative in your own field of expertise.

But our workplaces rarely provide an ideal environment for deep focus. And the norms around leadership, especially in a corporate environment, do not support taking time out of our day or week for deep focus. This is why many leaders do deep-focus work on their own time — at home, on the weekend, in the bath. I want you to have deep relaxation in the bath, not deep focus!

I worked with the senior partner from a prominent law firm once who told me of an experience he had as a junior lawyer. His managing partner walked into his office one day, catching him deep in thought, staring out of the window, which overlooked a stunning view of Sydney Harbour. My client jumped up on noticing the partner behind him and apologised profusely for staring out the window instead of slaving over the file on his desk. The senior partner's response was: 'Never be afraid to spend your time thinking. That is what we pay you for.'

The partner recognised that he was not slacking off enjoying the view — he was working on a problem in his head. My client was lucky to learn this early in his career, and passed it on over the years to younger lawyers he mentored.

The first thing we need to do if we want to incorporate deep focus into our way of working is to give ourselves permission to do it. To not feel guilty that we are slacking off or letting others down because we are not available for yet another meeting. We need to have conviction in our decisions about how we use our time.

So, what about when we really need to go deep on something? How do we create the space, the environment and the discipline to immerse ourselves and produce something of real value?

As I write this, I am in a process of deep focus. I have taken myself up the coast for the day, and allowed myself a day of no meetings, no emails and no distractions from this task. I am in an environment that is relaxing, good for concentrating and allows for a few rewards like a swim or a nice meal to help me recharge between intense writing periods. I have planned this time in my schedule and have fought fiercely to protect the time.

Don't feel that deep focus requires a full day or more away from the office. This is the sort of time allocation that I need to write books, and I need to plan these days into my schedule weeks or months in advance. If you don't have the luxury that Bill Gates has when spending his infamous think weeks in his remote shack a few times a year, don't think that you can't commit to deep focus. Deep focus can be an hour, a couple of hours or half a day protected on a Friday. But to achieve it, we need to commit to it.

Deep focus commitments

Deep focus requires commitment. In fact, it requires four commitments. These are commitments that we make to ourselves, as we are usually our own worst enemy when it comes to protecting our space for deep focus.

Commitment 1: Commit to a defined topic

I find it helpful if you go into a period of deep focus with a defined topic in mind. This aids your ability to focus and to achieve an outcome. Get some clarity about what success would look like at the end of the focus period. Set yourself a goal and work hard to achieve it.

The value of deep focus is you get to concentrate deeply on something worthwhile. When I put the full weight of my attention on a topic, issue or idea, great things usually happen.

If we compare applying the full weight of your attention on a topic versus attending yet another urgent meeting or getting a few emails flicked on, there should be no competition. You are a leader, so commit to doing what leaders should do!

Commitment 2: Commit to a time

If you are like many of the leaders I work with, you don't have too many gaps in your schedule over the next week or so. In order to have the space for focus work, you need to protect time before your schedule fills up. I am a fan of protecting three blocks of two hours in my schedule each week for 'focus time'. I plan these two weeks beforehand, but I don't specify what I am going to focus on in these blocks until I get closer to that week. These are simply placeholders to protect my time from other meetings. When I do my weekly planning the Friday before, I will get more specific about what I am going to use the time for.

It is critical that you are disciplined in protecting the time for focus activities. Many people protect time in their schedule, only to give it away cheaply as seemingly pressing meetings come their way, or they chew the focus time up with less valuable activities like email. When you truly commit to focus time, you follow through and focus on something worthwhile. Squandering this precious time is like diligently saving your hard-earned money only to blow it on fast food!

Commitment 3: Commit to minimising distractions

To focus deeply, you have to minimise distractions, both external and internal. The external ones are things like emails, interruptions and phone calls. Put your phone on silent, turn off your email, turn on your out-of-office auto-responder, if appropriate, and locate yourself in a place that will minimise interruptions from your team and colleagues. Book a meeting room or work from home. Be deliberate about this time.

You also need to manage the internal distractions. It can be hard to focus when other things are pulling at your mind. I tend to spend a bit of time before a focus period clearing the decks of any critical issues that may pull on my mind. This may involve dealing with any critical emails in your inbox or ticking a few tasks off my list so I can comfortably settle into my focus work for the next hour, few hours or day.

Commitment 4: Commit to staying the course

Focus can be hard. For some, you get into the flow and the time flies by. For others, it can be hard to get fully immersed. Either way, you need to find a way to get into a state of flow. Know what helps you concentrate. I find music is good for my concentration, although many don't. My friend Alex likes the background noise of a café for his deep focus. I find that rewards are also a good motivator for me. My reward after writing this will be a swim and a beer. A man of simple needs! But I always try to find a way to get started, and to keep going until I achieve a reasonable result in the time available. I've also got a few tricks up my sleeve to ease into the work and stay the course.

Immersing yourself in the work

I think of immersing myself in deep work a bit like easing myself into a hot spa. I have been to a few hot natural springs in places like New Zealand, and they are hot! You can't just jump in; they require a more subtle approach. So does focus work — it needs you to lower yourself into it slowly, and probably requires you to come out to cool off every now and again.

My Uncle Patrick is a retired journalist who started his career during the Vietnam War. He had a long career with some big publications, sometimes lunching or golfing with presidents and celebrities. One tip that he gave me many years ago was that when he was writing an article, he would finish a writing session mid-sentence. This meant that when he came back to focus on the article, he just had to finish the sentence and he was off again. This was his way to ease himself into the hot water.

Find your way to ease yourself in. Review where you last left off the work in question. Read something that will give you context and spark your thinking. Plan the focus session and the goals you want to achieve. Invest 10 per cent of your time in easing yourself in and you will be deeply immersed quickly. Be aware that you may need to take breaks to allow yourself to maintain focus.

When I research or write, I tend to focus deeply for periods of about 40 minutes to an hour, but need to come out of the hot water for a short while before immersing myself again. This is not just to take a break, but it helps me assimilate the information I have been dealing with. Writing can be a very blinkered activity, and a short break over a coffee, a walk or just doing a few emails allows me to relax my brain and think about the content with a bit more perspective. I then immerse myself again with more clarity and reinvigorated focus. By chance, as I was writing this chapter, I noticed that the Windows clock on my PC has been updated with a really handy focus timer that allows me to set a time to concentrate. It sits in the top corner of the screen, counting down and also reminding me to take a break. Microsoft are really thinking about how they bring ideas like these to life for us.

In a busy leader's role, it can be very challenging to protect time for this type of deep focus. But it is, in part, what you get paid to do. It is the value that you as a leader and a senior mind in your business can provide. Fight for this time, and don't just be a victim of your schedule and bend to doing some of your most valuable work on your own time. This is how you can have more impact, which will be our topic in the next chapter.

Reflections and intentions

- Do you struggle with wide focus?

- Do you struggle with deep focus?

- What are you going to do differently to manage your focus?

- What environments do you have access to for deep focus?

- Think about your preferred productivity style (Organiser, Energiser, Analyser). How does your style impact your ability to focus wide and deep?

CHAPTER 4
Have more impact

In my introduction, I posed the question 'Are you a leader who is too busy to lead?' If the answer to this question is 'yes', that kind of hurts, doesn't it? Your role as a leader should be inspirational, transformational, impactful. This should be the whole point of our existence as a leader in the workplace. We should be investing most of our time, energy and focus doing things that are transformational for the team and the work the team delivers to the rest of the organisation, clients or stakeholders.

The reality of our busy workplaces is that they put pressure on us to get work done, and when resources are tight, as they often are, we as leaders feel the need to roll up our sleeves and muck in with our busy team. This is an excellent thing to do as a leader in exceptional circumstances, but when it becomes the norm, we have a problem. If this happens, we are getting dragged down below the line.

Get above the line

In their book *15 Commitments of Conscious Leadership*, Jim Dethmer, Diana Chapman and Kaley Warner Klemp talk about the concept of leaders leading from 'above the line'. They say that a leader is leading from above the line when they are open, curious and committed to learning, but they are leading from below the line when they are closed, defensive and committed to being right. Their argument is that, while we all work below the line sometimes, we are more effective leaders when we are above the line.

It is such a simple and elegant concept, which they go on to back up with 15 strategies for leaders to use to work from above the line. One of the most powerful related ideas is that the key to self-awareness is to know if you are operating above or below the line. They say that *knowing* you are below the line is more important than the fact that you *are* below the line. Many leaders, when asked whether they lead from above or below the line, delude themselves into thinking they are leading from above the line, as they see below the line as being 'wrong'.

I feel this idea has relevance to our productivity as well. When I work with leaders on their personal productivity, and specifically on the impact they have, we talk about above and below the line. I believe that when we are working above the line, we are focused on the activities that only we, as a leader, can do, as well as the activities that are transformational for our team. When we are below the line, we might be busy, but we are busy doing work that takes us away from what is above the line. This work is not necessarily a waste of time, and I am sure it needs to be done, but there is an opportunity cost.

When we are working above the line, we are focused on the activities that only we, as a leader, can do, as well the activities that are transformational for our team.

It is fairly black and white — when we are below the line, we are not above the line. And it is a choice we make, consciously or unconsciously. This is the opportunity cost inherent in our busy lives. You only have a finite amount of time, energy and focus to give to the different aspects of your role, your life and yourself.

An even bigger challenge presents itself when we delude ourselves that we are being productive in our role because we are busy. If we do not have the self-awareness to know we are below the line, we cannot do anything to shift this and get back above the line as soon as possible. So, self-awareness is the first step.

How can we tell if we are above the line? We need to make what is above the line in our role explicit, then take some time to map out what activities and priorities are above the line for us. While we are at it, we need to define the things that commonly drag us down below the line.

Stay in your lane

Many years ago, I received some priceless mentoring from a friend. He had been running a highly successful business for 20 years, and believed my training business had a huge amount of potential that was perhaps not being realised. He told me that he saw how I worked, and while I was highly organised, I was not necessarily focusing on the right things. This was his version of the above the line/below the line idea.

He helped me to map out four areas that I should concentrate my time, energy and focus on to grow my training business in a sustainable way. For me, these became four groups of activity that I focus on most of the time: *think, sell, deliver* and *team*.

I manage my time around these key areas, and think of them as the lanes in which I need to keep to if I am maximising my impact. I need time to *think*, which includes activities like developing ideas and writing. I need time to *sell* what we do to key clients. I need time to *deliver* training and keynote speeches. And I need time to lead my *team*.

This is not rocket science, but just visualising these four areas of impact helped me stay in my lanes. It increased my self-awareness and allowed me to question many activities that consumed my time, asking if they were in one of my four lanes. If not, I worked on doing something about it. We will look at this on page 84.

A number of years after this mentoring conversation, I was exposed to the 'above the line concept' and overlaid it on my four lanes. This allowed me to define the activities that would fall into the four lanes, but were below the line for me (maybe not for someone else though). It also helped me to clarify what was above the line for me.

A good example of this is training delivery. I have been running my training practice for over 20 years. For many of those years, delivering training, any training, was a good use of my time. But as my practice grew, and our productivity offerings became more sophisticated, I was finding that I was very busy delivering training, but not all of it was the best use of *my* time. A lot of it was Smart Work training being rolled out across teams in our client organisations. This could be run by my team, but often the client wanted me, purely because I was the face of the business and the author of the book.

The opportunity cost for me was that I was not available to deliver conference keynotes or Lead Smart training because I was booked out for months in advance delivering Smart Work. Now you could say that any work is good work, don't complain. But it is not. It is far better for my clients if I am personally deployed to engage the leadership level, to transform their thinking, rather than deliver the core training that my team can deliver just as well as I can.

When I mapped out the activities in *think, sell, deliver* and *team* that were above the line for me and below the line for me, I became highly self-aware and changed how I prioritised my time, energy and focus (see figure 4.1). This transformed the results I was achieving, and helped me grow the business that my mentor had envisioned that day many years before. And it helped me to do it in a sustainable way, with healthy work/life balance, with a focus on the work that inspired me the most.

Why not have a go at identifying your lanes, and what might be above and below the line in each? All you need is a pen, a piece of paper and a strong coffee.

First of all, work out what your lanes might be. What are the four or five areas of your role that define your most impactful activities? Maybe take a look at your goals and objectives, or your 'key result area' document if that is how you measure activity and performance in your role. (Four is the number of lanes that works for my role. You may end up with five, or three, which is absolutely fine).

Next, jot down the specific types of activities that you should be spending more of your time, energy and focus on. These will go above the line. Finally, outline the things that typically drag you below the line. We will look at some strategies that you can apply to minimise these next.

If you feel brave enough once you have done this exercise, take a look at your schedule and active priorities and see how they stack up. Is what you have already committed to above the line or below the line? What will you do about it? What can you do about it? Let's look at that next.

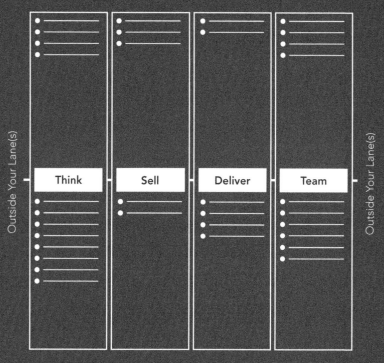

Figure 4.1: Defining your lanes

Five strategies to get above the line

If you have done some analysis and found that you are below the line more than you might like, what can you do? Rather than taking a knee-jerk reaction approach to this problem — cancelling everything or dumping a pile of stuff on your team — try to apply one or more of the following strategies. You can choose to shift work, shrink it, simplify it, suspend it, or even stop it (see figure 4.2). You have agency and the choice is yours.

Shift	Shrink	Simplify
Give it away	Make it smaller	Make it easier

Suspend	Stop
Pause it temporarily	End it permanently

Figure 4.2: Strategies to get above the line

1. Shift: Give it away

There are bound to be a number of activities in your calendar, in your task list or in your inbox that you could shift to someone else — someone whose time, energy and focus is better deployed on the activity. We will talk about delegation in more detail in chapter 6, with lots of strategies around how and when you delegate. But delegate you must.

Now, you are probably thinking about how much you already delegate, and like the leaders discussed in the *15 Commitments of*

Conscious Leadership, you may be committed to being right and deluding yourself that you delegate the appropriate amount. The truth is, though, you probably don't and are not ruthless enough about it. You tell yourself stories about how busy your team is, that this is just a crazy period that requires you to be hands-on, how they won't do it right anyway, and that you might as well do it yourself as it will take just as long to delegate it. All 'below the line' mindsets.

2. Shrink: Make it smaller

If delegation is not an option, but you deem the task to be outside your lane, or below the line, you might be able to shrink the activity to a smaller scale that requires less of your time, energy or focus. If it is a meeting, could it be shorter or a quick discussion rather than a formal meeting? If it is a task, is there part of the task that you can do that is above the line, and part of it that can be done by others? Question each activity and be creative in getting yourself above the line.

3. Simplify: Make it easier

Is there a way that the complex work that demands a lot of your time, energy or focus could be made simpler? Is there a process that could be redesigned to make it simpler in the future? Is there friction that could be removed in the execution of the task that makes it easier for you to get it done? Could you request an executive summary to summarise the complex report you need to review?

4. Suspend: Pause it temporarily

Is there an activity that, under normal circumstances, would be a great use of your time, but due to other pressures is not the best use of your time right now? Could this activity be scheduled for later, and picked up again when you come back up for air. Because I use a dated task list, with the ability to schedule a task for any chosen day, I tend to use my task list on the first day of each month to capture things that I don't want to forget completely, but cannot focus on this month due to other priorities.

5. Stop: End it permanently

Finally, what are the things you do that you just should not be doing, and in fact, should not be done at all? What are the things that might have been relevant a year ago, but are no longer relevant, and are still being done because no one thought to question them? This is your opportunity to question them.

● ● ●

If you want to stay above the line, you need to actively manage your time, energy and focus. You have to be purposeful and intentional. You have to be ruthless. Ultimately it will come down to how you prioritise the allocation of your resources, so let's have a talk about prioritisation.

Prioritisation strategies

When I talk to leadership teams about how they prioritise their work on a day-to-day basis, they can find it hard to verbalise their methodology. Prioritisation is often intuitive, and if they do have a methodology, they usually reference Eisenhower's matrix, which combines the elements of urgency and importance and prescribes strategies for the four different combinations you may be faced with. Important and urgent, not important and not urgent, and so on.

In today's busy and often reactive workplace, I have noticed a particular confusion set in around what the word 'importance' means. Many people will say that something is important, but what they really mean is that it is urgent. They are confusing time-sensitivity with impact and value.

This is the formula I discuss in my training when I talk about prioritisation:

$$Urgency \times Importance = Priority$$

This statement makes sense to most people, and is definitely in line with Eisenhower's matrix. Every piece of work has some level of urgency, and some level of import attached to it. Here is the problem. For me this equation may be correct, but it is the wrong way around. In a workplace that prides itself on work that is valuable and important, the equation should read:

$$Importance \times Urgency = Priority$$

Because of the pace of today's busy workplace, we have slowly but surely fallen into the trap of using urgency as the first (and sometimes only) filter we assess priorities through, rather than an importance filter. It becomes a default where we ask ourselves whether something is urgent, rather than having the confidence and conviction to first ask if it is *important.*

The first approach might be OK at more junior levels within the team. This assumes that the leadership team is making good decisions about priorities on their workers' behalf as they delegate work. But at the leadership level, we must always try to put importance first when assessing incoming work.

We talked about how critical proactive planning is in balancing inputs and outcomes in chapter 2. If you are making time for regular personal planning, you should be driving the right work into your schedule, which is an 'importance first' strategy. But you also need to complement that with an 'importance first' strategy for the urgent inputs that come at you daily: meeting invites, task requests and emails. We need to resist the urge to react in a knee-jerk way. Knee-jerk reactions, where a doctor hits you on the knee with a hammer, causing it to jerk upwards, bypass the brain and any conscious decision-making, and instead react to the direct stimulus. I wonder if we do the same thing with some of our work — simply react without thought or conscious decision-making taking place?

Three distinct prioritisation strategies

So what prioritisation methodologies can we implement to help ourselves and our team make good decisions in each moment about what is the best use of their resources? I find the following three methods easy to remember and easy to use, like tools in my kitbag. One uses an importance lens, one an urgency lens, and the last a combination.

Filtering

Just like a good chef will strain a stock through a muslin cloth to filter out the lumps and impurities, a good leader should run every invite, request, email and interruption through a filter that only lets the right work through. In *Smart Work,* I talk about the four actions you can take with an email: dump, divert, decide when, and do it now. This is a priority filter, and should ensure that only the important stuff ends up in your calendar or task list. Of course, this doesn't need to be restricted to emails; it can be applied to any form of input.

The key is to be ruthless and decisive at the point of entry. Don't let stuff that should not be there build up in your inbox — make decisions and move it out. And don't let stuff get through that should not be there. A good example of this is allowing meetings to creep into your schedule, only to look at your schedule for the week and baulk at your busyness or kick yourself for saying 'yes' in the first place. Being more ruthless at the point of entry saves you time and angst down the track.

When we filter well, we end up doing the *right work*, because we are asking the importance question first.

Scheduling

Many people scratch their head when I suggest that scheduling is a prioritisation technique. But if you think about it, once work has gotten through your initial filter, the assumption is that you have decided it is a good use of your time. So the next question is, when am I going to do it? By scheduling activities in our calendar or a dated task list, we are making priority decisions. If I decide to schedule something for next Tuesday rather than today, I am prioritising how I allocate my time.

This is why it is so crucial for you to have a date-based task system in place to manage your priorities. You need to use your time holistically to get both your meeting workload and your task workload done in a timely way. Any system that does not allow you to manage your priorities within the context of your time, limits your ability to prioritise.

Scheduling helps me to do the *right work at the right time*, and has more of a focus on urgency than importance. This is appropriate because I have already run it through the importance filter.

Ranking

Finally, the ability to rank or sequence a list is a really useful tool to help concentrate your focus on what is most critical. I rank my daily task list by dragging tasks up and down to create a ranking from most important to least important. I rank a list of my monthly 'top ten' priorities from most important to least important, so that I have a clear view of my top big-picture priorities for each month. I rank meeting agendas from most important to least important so that we attack the critical stuff first.

One very senior executive that I worked with at Walmart International in the US, who was responsible for many hundreds of thousands of staff, told me that her strategy for juggling numerous competing priorities was always knowing her top three priorities. She used an informal ranking technique to identify her top three priorities for each month, and expected her extended leadership team to do the same, and be able to share them confidently at any time. She told me that this was one of the things she did to create an importance-driven culture. My realisation after that conversation was that this exercise not only gave her and her team clarity, but it also gave them the confidence and conviction to fight for their priorities, and have respectful but robust negotiations when priority conflicts arose.

When ranking a list, you will probably use a combination of importance and urgency to make your ranking decisions, but you will definitely end up doing the *right work, at the right time, with the right focus.*

Create a red velvet rope policy

I reckon we all need a red velvet rope policy. I am going to talk about this idea within the context of your meeting workload, as I believe that too many meetings is a problematic issue for leaders, as they end up with overfull, compressed schedules and little space for anything else. So I like to link this to your meeting workload, but you can apply this concept to any activity. It is also very closely aligned to the 'above the line' concept we discussed earlier.

When I was in my early twenties in Dublin in the 1990s, myself and my mates would hit the town on the weekend. On a typical Friday or Saturday night, we'd all head off to the local disco after the pub, which would usually close at about 1 am. If we were in the mood for a really big night, we would pile into a taxi and head to Leeson St, which was the dodgy 'red light' area in the city centre. This is where the nightclubs that opened until 6 am were, full of drunk revellers, fuelled up on cheap bubbly and orange juice.

The challenge was, they were pretty hard to get into when you were a 22-year-old, slightly inebriated male. There was usually a big bouncer on the door, and they always had a red velvet rope strung across two brass poles barring the entrance. Now, if you were Bono, they lifted the rope quick smart and let you in. If you were a beautiful model, entry was assured. But if you were me, the red velvet rope stayed firmly in place most of the time, along with the line, 'Sorry, we're full'. Every bloody Friday!

These bouncers had what I call a 'strict red velvet rope policy'. They were very discerning about who they let into their clubs, and they could be, because there was way more demand than there was room in the club. The same is true of your schedule: there is way more demand than time available. So be prepared to keep that red velvet rope in place more of the time when you receive meeting requests. This is a prioritisation decision, and you should always evaluate the opportunity cost, even if you are available at the proposed time. When our schedule fills up, it can be hard to remain flexible for the priorities or opportunities that can arise.

One of my senior coaching clients shared a personal experience with me that became the inspiration for this book. He was sharing with me why he had taken the plunge to invest his budget and time in working with me one-on-one to re-engineer his approach to productivity. Andy was a senior executive in a large organisation, working about two levels below the CEO. One day he bumped into the CEO in the hallway, and the CEO was really pleased to see him and have the chance to check in with him. In fact, he said to Andy, 'We should catch up properly for a coffee'. Andy saw this as a great opportunity, and suggested he get his EA to reach out to the CEO's EA to make a time. The CEO replied 'No, let's make a time now. I have some space this afternoon.'

Andy got out his phone, and as he scrolled through his packed schedule, a sick feeling crept up from his belly. He was not available that afternoon; in fact, he could not find a free spot in his schedule for nearly a month! He told the CEO he would try to shift something, but would have to get back and confirm with him.

Now I am sure Andy made it happen in the end — he would be crazy not to. But he told me that this was a real moment for him, where he realised that the CEO was operating at a different level to him. The CEO had more capacity and flexibility than he had! What was going on here? (Remember the meeting workload curve on page 44?) Andy came to me soon after and wanted to work on how to shift his way of working so that he was ready for the next level of seniority before he got there. He wanted to level up as the CEO obviously had.

● ● ●

Levelling up your personal productivity is one of the most powerful things you can do as a leader. When you maximise your time, energy and focus, you create more impact for your organisation. But an even more powerful action is to upgrade how you work with your team, and how you help them to be their most productive selves. That is a highly leveraged and impactful project for any leader. In part II and part III of the book we will look at a range of strategies that you can apply to leverage the productivity of those around you.

Reflections and intentions

- How clear are you about your 'lanes'?

- What activities would be 'above the line' in your role?

- Are you spending enough of your time, energy and focus on the things that are above the line in your lanes?

- What typically drags you below the line?

- Think about your preferred productivity style (Organiser, Energiser, Analyser). How does your style impact your ability to work above the line and have impact as a leader?

PART II
TEAM INTERFACE

The *Cambridge Dictionary* describes the word interface as 'a situation, way, or place where two things come together and affect each other'. You can imagine that for the two parts coming together, a successful interface would often mean that there is a strong connection between them. If there is a mismatch, then they will not connect well. Think about two surfaces being glued together – they need to both be prepared in a way that allows for a good bond. Or imagine the hook and loop components on a Velcro fastener. They are different surfaces, but they bond well with each other because they are complimentary.

Likewise, the interface between you and your team needs to be solid, clean and complimentary, otherwise productivity friction is created.

Working together

The Hippocratic Oath, or the doctor's creed, has doctors and surgeons swear to do no harm to the patients they work with. What a good mindset to bring to how we work with our team, especially those whom we work most closely with, those in our direct line of sight, and those at risk of having their productivity disrupted by our behaviours. We need to recognise that, as leaders, we can be extremely disruptive to the productivity of our team, whether it is intentional or not.

And it cuts both ways. Our direct team can be extremely disruptive to our productivity if we let them; however, if you work with them to ensure the interface between you is productive rather than disruptive, everyone wins. But it all starts with you, the leader. Elite-level productivity radiates outwards in a spiral from you, the leader, through your executive support, to your direct reports, to the wider team, and beyond to other parts of the business and your personal life (see figure C, overleaf).

Conversely, if your productivity habits and routines are not operating at an elite level, you could be infecting those around you with unclear expectations, poorly modelled behaviours and productivity friction. Be careful, the spiral can be positive or negative.

Setting up good co-working habits and routines with your team will help you get more done through them. As a team, when you proactively work to develop how you communicate with each other, how you delegate or escalate work, how you conduct 1:1 catch-ups and how you align yourselves behind key priorities, you become a highly effective unit that gets stuff done.

So, this section of the book will specifically look at how you interface with your team, and the productivity partnerships you build to increase effectiveness and reduce friction. We will start with how you work with your EA or PA, if relevant. I understand that not all leaders will have the luxury of dedicated executive support these days. Even if your team has a team assistant, it is worth thinking about how you work with them.

We will then look at how you operate with your direct reports, and how you coach them to operate with their teams. And finally we will look at how you interface with the wider team.

Figure C: The elite productivity spiral

CHAPTER 5

Leverage your support

There is a group of people who you work closely with who are absolutely essential to your productivity. Depending on your leadership role, and the organisation you work in, this group may include your EA (for simplicity's sake, I am going to refer to your assistant as an EA, although they may hold another title), your direct leadership team or your direct reports. These are the people who are most likely to have either a positive or negative impact on your productivity, so it is really worthwhile to put some explicit strategies in place for how you will all work together.

Some organisations still believe in the value of senior executives having dedicated EA support. Other organisations have stripped this out except for the most senior roles. Some have moved to a team assistant model, where one person supports the whole leadership team. In this next part, I am assuming you have a dedicated EA, and are in a position to craft a way of working with them that is beneficial for both you and them. If you do not have an EA, feel free to skip ahead to page 114 where I discuss how you interface with your direct reports.

Productive EA strategies

Having worked with many senior leaders over the years, I have also worked with their EAs. Sometimes we work as a small group, sometimes I am working with the executive, and sometimes I am working 1:1 with the EA. When I have some alone time with the EA, they are often quite frank about the frustrations they experience trying to juggle a busy leader's schedule and commitments. They are always extremely loyal, and usually love supporting their exec, but three common frustrations are often aired.

Firstly, they often struggle with the leader not saying 'no' to meetings, and just expecting the EA to magically fit more meetings into an already ridiculous schedule. Some EAs spend half their time just moving and removing existing meetings to fit in the seemingly 'urgent' new meetings that need to be squeezed in.

The second frustration is not being able to easily understand what is going on in the executive's overflowing inbox, with much confusion over what has been dealt with already, what is a priority and where emails should be filed if they are to be retained. An inbox with thousands of emails in it is impossible for anyone to make sense of.

Finally, there is often a frustration that time spent catching up with the EA is not prioritised, and catch-ups get constantly cancelled or moved. It is very hard for the EA to do the job of keeping the leader organised and working on the right stuff if they never get to interface with them, or when they do, it is a half-baked five minutes moving between one meeting and another.

If you are lucky enough to have an EA, treasure them, and help them to help you. They can amplify your effectiveness if you set up the partnership in the right way.

When I started out running my own training company, it was just me. In the first couple of years, I was not so busy that I couldn't handle it myself, and realistically, I couldn't afford to hire an EA. But after a while, I got busier, and the advice from my mentors was to hire an EA now, rather than waiting until later.

Of course, I did not listen. I was a productivity expert, highly organised and I felt I could do it all myself. But as my business continued to grow, I hit a ceiling that I could not seem to push past, and just ended up working more and more, trying to do everything myself. I eventually saw the light, and hired Chauntelle as a part-time assistant. She is now my business manager, and absolutely central to my and the business's success. It was only after I created a productive partnership with her that I realised how much I had held myself back in the early years, telling myself that I could do it all myself.

The truth is, I am a better writer, a better trainer, a better thinker, a better speaker and a better leader because of her support. But this is not just about having another pair of hands to do the work. This is about working above the line, and having someone who can get inside my head to understand what is needed, and do many of the below the line things for me that need to be done.

Chauntelle sees her role as a simple one. Every day she aims to make my life easier, and to remove friction for me. Simple. But to achieve those things, we need to have an excellent working understanding. This starts with understanding how my role and hers fit together. Working with your EA is the first productivity partnership you need to work on.

Two sides of the same coin

The partnership that you have with your EA will, to some extent, depend on their capability and ability to step up to meet your needs. But it is also highly dependent on what you bring to the partnership, and how you coach them to work with you. I see the leader and the EA as two sides of the same coin. You both have a part to play in keeping you, the leader, organised.

A good starting point is to ensure that your EA removes friction for you, or at the very least, does not generate friction for you. A poor exec/EA partnership will create productivity friction, with mistakes being made, meetings being double-booked, work needing to be redone and things being forgotten. A good exec/EA partnership will avoid productivity friction, with things being done in a timely and acceptable manner. But a great exec/EA partnership will remove productivity friction altogether, as problems are anticipated and avoided, and proactive strategies put in place to make the executive's life easier. Notice I did not say a great EA, but a great partnership. Your EA, no matter how good they are, can only do so much if your ways of working leave a lot to be desired. This is something you need to work on together.

I see the leader and the EA as two sides of the same coin. You both have a part to play in keeping you, the leader, organised.

One of the ingredients that will need to be present if you want to make this partnership great, is to have an active EA versus a passive EA. I get to deal with a lot of EAs, PAs and team assistants in my role working with leadership teams. They are usually highly organised, and pride themselves on this. But one of the differences between good and great for me is whether they are active or passive. Passive EAs can do what they are asked to do in an efficient and timely way. But an active EA goes beyond this — they actively engage to anticipate what the executive needs, as well as what their team needs, and they work to clear the path for the executive to work above the line as much of the time as possible.

Some examples of the approach an active EA would take are:

- organising a meeting and protecting some time for you to review the papers beforehand

- anticipating your needs when travelling interstate

- evaluating the need for you to attend a meeting and possibly declining on your behalf

- responding to a request to do something with, 'Already done'

- while you are in meetings, responding to an important email in your inbox and arranging a next-step action to get things moving.

Being active versus passive requires experience, it requires confidence and it requires trust. This all comes with time and some work. If you are hiring an EA, this is something to look for. Can they demonstrate examples of how they have actively anticipated the needs of previous executives they have supported? Or are they stuck in a passive paradigm, able to do what is asked of them, but no more? If it is the latter, this will always limit and frustrate you.

This is something that you and your current EA can work on together. Debriefing issues when they arise, and discussing what could be done differently next time is a key strategy. The more experience they get working with you, the more they can get inside your head. And the more inside your head they can see, the better they can anticipate your needs or the decision you would most likely take in certain situations.

In your productivity partnership, you both play a role in keeping you, the leader, as productive as possible. You'll likely have less available time than your EA, because your schedule and priority list are, by nature, more pressured. (If this is not the case, some deep examination should be conducted!) But you hold the expertise of being a leader. Not to say your EA does not have expertise, but your expertise as a leader is what we need to maximise here, and is the reason you have an EA in the first place (see figure 5.1, overleaf).

Your EA does not have the same level of executive expertise as you, but in the context of being the flip side of your coin, they do have more time. They have the capacity to get so much done on your behalf, but only if they understand what needs to be done, which requires some direction from you or some insight into your thinking. The time that they have available to do things on your behalf will be wasted if they are simply waiting for you to have the time to delegate stuff to them.

Let's have a look at some ways that you could create a super-productive partnership with your EA—one that serves you both. I would assume that your EA has many duties in the organisation of you, but the key ones will likely be managing your schedule and associated information; helping to manage

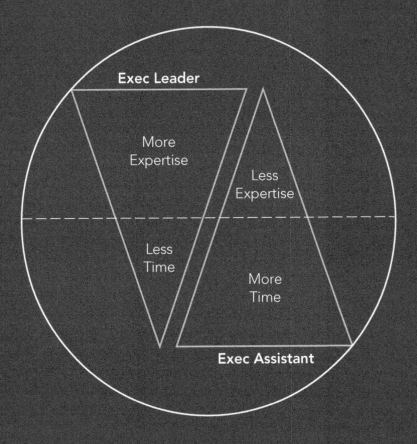

Figure 5.1: Two sides of the same coin

your inbox; acting as a buffer between your wider team and you, indeed, the wider organisation and you; as well as operational things, such as travel and approvals. They may even manage certain projects for you, at least from a technical point of view. Why don't we start with your calendar and schedule?

Is your schedule self-driven or chauffeur-driven?

One of the key duties in your EA's role should be managing your calendar and schedule. This does not mean that they manage your time! You need to manage your own time, and that means you have to take an active role in what goes into your schedule. But they will manage a lot of the mechanics and moving parts in your schedule.

The first thing you will need to decide is whether you want to be self-driven or chauffeur-driven. By this I mean, will they take most of the control over inputting, moving and removing things from your calendar, or will you do this yourself? The choice is yours, but my advice is to make a decision and stick to it. When you have a chauffeur in the driver's seat, but you insist on sitting in the passenger seat with one hand on the wheel, chaos ensues!

If you have a dedicated EA, it makes sense to let them control the mechanics of your schedule, making sure you both have regular discussions about what is in your schedule and why. I tend to avoid putting anything but personal meetings into my own schedule. If a client wants to book a time with me, I always get Chauntelle involved as she is much better at making sure the time chosen is the optimal time. She is also better at being objective than I am, and will not give my time away cheaply. If it were left up to me, I would say 'yes' to far too many things!

If you decide that you want to be chauffeur-driven, then give your EA full authority over your schedule. If people approach you directly to arrange a time to meet, always direct them back through your EA to make the arrangements. If you don't do this, you are giving people a back door to sneak into your schedule through, making your EA's life harder.

For your EA to manage your schedule fully, they must have full visibility of your priorities as well. Most EAs I have worked with over the years have told me they have full visibility of their executive's calendar, but no visibility of their priorities and tasks. How on earth can they help the exec manage or protect their time if they cannot see what they need time for?

As we looked at in chapter 3, having your task list in MS Outlook, or whatever scheduling tool you are using, is a good idea. At least then your EA can get a sense of your total workload for the week. If this is not possible, having a regular discussion about what is coming up, including what priorities you have on your plate, will give them the wider context they need to help you organise your time fully.

Using some sort of coding system in your calendar can be useful too. Many leaders use categories in their calendar to colour code their appointments. This gives context and meaning. If you do this, be sure to share what each colour means with your EA, and make sure they consistently use these colours so you (and they) can get that context at a glance.

Using the Free, Working Elsewhere, Tentative, Busy, Out of Office field on calendar entries can also bring useful meaning to your calendar. If you have time blocked out in your calendar to review a report, you might make that time Tentative, so your EA knows it is negotiable. If you have a personal appointment in your calendar, it may be worth marking it as Out of Office to indicate that it is not negotiable, and you will not even be in the building.

Consider giving your EA permission to speak with your 'voice' in negotiations around your schedule. In a coaching call with an exec and their EA, it became obvious that the EA got a lot of pressure from senior stakeholders in the business to fit last-minute meetings into the exec's already busy schedule. She found it hard to respectfully say no. In our coaching call, we agreed that the EA had the exec's full permission to say something along the lines of: 'Amanda does not have the capacity to fit meetings into her busy schedule at the last minute. I am happy to make a time for you to meet her, but it will need to be next week.' This takes confidence, and the executive needs to inject that confidence into the EA by giving them permission to speak with their voice. Again, this sort of confidence is the sign of an active EA.

Finally, having a talk with your EA about what is above the line for you and what is below the line for you, as mapped out in chapter 4, will help them organise your schedule more effectively. When you give them this context, they are far better able to make good decisions about the meetings you want to make it into your calendar, and the meetings that you don't. Or the meetings that need 45 minutes versus the ones that should be switched to a ten-minute conversation.

Making your inbox a meaningful co-working space

Not every executive wants their EA to have access or control over their email, though I think this should be a no-brainer. Allow them to help you, and trust them to deal with the information in your inbox appropriately and respectfully. This is a partnership after all. Again, it would be a good idea to decide if you are going to be a self-driver or want to be chauffeur-driven with your inbox, although there is more scope for the two of you to share the driving in this case. You just need to be really clear about it.

A common complaint that I hear from EAs is that they have no idea what is going on in their exec's inbox. They are often looking at an inbox that contains many thousands of emails, some read, some unread, some flagged, some not, some finished with and some still active. It can be hard to know where to start if the EA wants to help manage the deluge.

Executives who keep their inbox down to the few emails that they have not dealt with yet make it much easier for their EA to understand which ones are still an open topic. Executives who use a simple filing system for emails make it much easier for their EA to file informational emails on their behalf, and even to find emails for them if they are in a meeting or away from their computer.

If an executive has 126 filing folders, and the EA has to guess which folder they would have filed an email into, it can be a daunting task. But if they just use one filing folder to store the emails they want to keep, the EA can do a search in that folder and is far more likely to find the email quickly. And when it comes to filing emails, the EA can easily do this as they don't need to decipher the exec's thinking process to file the email, they just file it into the one folder! So easy.

When it comes to processing emails, there are a few of models you could go with.

- You are a self-driver, and you process all of your own emails. This could just be your preference, or may be driven by the fact that there may be sensitive emails in your inbox for your eyes only. I would think very carefully about this approach though, as it will drag you below the line.

- You are chauffeur-driven, and let your EA process the bulk of your emails, only leaving the few that require your attention, which you might deal with at the end of the day/week.

- You share the driving, with you doing most of the driving, but your EA jumping in where necessary. Personally, most of the time I manage my own email, but when I am involved in an all-day training delivery with a client, Chauntelle will keep an eye on my email, highlighting anything critical for me, but dealing with a lot of it herself.

As I outlined in *Smart Work*, there are only four things you need to do with an email when you are processing your inbox. You can:

- *dump it* by deleting or filing it

- *divert it* by delegating or negotiating it

- *decide when* and schedule it as a task or time in your calendar

- *do it now.*

With a bit of experience and context, your EA would be able to do the first two of those actions for you, and dump or divert a lot of your inbox before you even see it. That just leaves the emails that need you to decide when to deal with them. Your EA might not be able to process your emails all the way to zero, but they can certainly reduce the volume and clutter that you don't need to see.

When you are processing your own emails, there will be emails that you need to delegate to your EA or discuss with them. Of course, you can forward the email on to them and ask them to action it. But there are a couple of additional strategies I would recommend for this. The first is to use a tool like OneNote to manage the email as a discussion item. You can send the email to OneNote and add it to your list of things to discuss in your 1:1 catch-up. I talk more about this strategy on page 115, as it is a critical strategy for your direct team as well.

The other option involves regular, repetitive work that you need to flick on to your EA. For these types of emails, I sometimes recommend using batching folders. For example, one leader I worked with has his EA arrange a lot of meetings for him, and would forward the email each time, requesting that she organise a meeting about the content of the email. He felt there was a lot of typing involved with this strategy, which was not his strong point, especially if he was using his phone. So we decided to set up a folder in his mailbox called 'Arrange meeting', and he would just move the email to that folder. His EA checked this folder throughout the day, and nine times out of ten, was clear about what needed to happen. It was easier for him, easy for her and worked pretty well.

A note on Cc emails. Many leaders I work with use a Cc email folder, and set up a rule to move any emails they have been Cc'd on into this folder to make their inbox more focused. I like this idea, as long as you do look at the Cc folder every couple of days when you have the time. In this case, it's not a bad idea for your EA to skim through your Cc emails each day to ensure there is nothing critical in there that may need your attention or action.

The exec/EA catch-up

The most important meeting in your week is the one you have with your EA. Yet, it is often the one you cancel to reclaim time for some other meeting or some important priority. But you may need to adjust your thinking on this. This catch-up is for your benefit, not just your EA's! You both lose out when you don't have that time to connect, delegate, make decisions and move work forward. So here is my mantra around this. We can *shift* it. We can *shorten* it. We can even *squeeze* it into a crack somewhere. But we cannot *skip* it if we can possibly avoid it!

I know, in my role, that not only does Chauntelle work better when we have our regular catch-up, but I move so many things off my plate when we catch up properly. I am not perfect at this, though; in fact, I skipped our catch-up just the other day, and am very conscious about that. This is an example of my self-awareness about when I am operating below the line, as I was in this instance. But that was an exceptional circumstance, and I will be sure not to make a habit of it. In fact, we have a rule that if the meeting does get skipped, it cannot be skipped twice in a row.

Your cadence around catching up with your EA will depend on your workstyle. I find that one catch-up per week is all we need, but we are a well-oiled machine with reasonably predictable work. Many of my senior clients in corporate land would catch up with their EA twice per week, or sometimes every day, depending on how quickly things shift in their schedules.

I strongly suggest that one of your catch-ups involve a weekly ROAR planning process. ROAR is a weekly planning process that I originally outlined in *Smart Work*:

- **R**eview last week
- **O**rganise next week
- **A**nticipate the next few weeks
- **R**ealign with the big picture.

So essentially, look back, look forward, look even further forward and then look up. This gives you a three-dimensional view of your world, and helps you to plan and organise everything that you need to do over the coming weeks.

I often try to do a ROAR with Chauntelle when we meet. She lives 200 km away from me, so our catch-ups are over a video call in MS Teams. But we can both look back at the week that I have just had, and make sure all next-step actions have been done, delegated or scheduled. (This is a great opportunity for me to delegate next-step actions to her that have dropped out of my meetings that week.)

We then organise the next week together in detail, thinking about both my meetings and my priorities. We protect time for key tasks in my calendar, and we ensure that I have all of the information I need to make my meetings productive.

We then scan four to six weeks ahead in my schedule, and start to anticipate upcoming deadlines, travel and commitments. This helps us both to think really proactively. Finally, we have a quick discussion about the bigger picture, especially my quarterly goals and any projects I am working on. This is our chance to drop important work into my schedule or task list, or even better, into hers.

The discussions that we have during this weekly ROAR are a great way to not only make visible what we both need to do, but to give Chauntelle the context she needs to be a more active EA.

Your direct reports

If you and your EA are the central hub of the productivity partnership, then your direct reports, or core leadership team, are the next ring out that sits between you and the wider team.

This is the second productivity partnership you need to build. These are the people who will be tasked with organising a lot of the work you need executed, and will manage the wider team under your direction. Some of the work they will do will flow from the yearly or quarterly plans and priorities that you set as an organisation and a team, and some will flow from you more directly as you go.

It is crucial that you have a productive working partnership with this group, and this is where there is the greatest risk of productivity friction for you (and them). These are the people that you need to be most closely aligned with, and the people you need to be able to trust to get the right work done.

How you communicate and meet with this group will make or break the productivity and performance at the pointy end of your team. So it is worth making sure you reduce the risk of productivity friction.

1:1 catch-ups

How you manage your 1:1 catch-ups is an important factor in how well you work together. Your cadence for 1:1s may be weekly, bi-weekly or even monthly. They should be reasonably regular though, and they should be focused. That is why, as touched upon earlier, I am a huge fan of leveraging tools like MS OneNote to manage 1:1 discussions.

I use a notebook in OneNote that I call '1:1 Discussions'. I have a section for each of my direct reports, with a master page that holds a list of things that I need to discuss with them. The basic idea behind using a system like this is to consistently capture things for discussion on this list. When I am at my desk and I think of something to discuss with one of the team, I quickly flick to their page and capture it on the list. When I am out and about, I grab my phone and capture it in the mobile version of OneNote, as it syncs with my desktop app.

To enhance the catch-ups even more, I share the notebook with my team, so they can also add the things they want to discuss with me. OneNote is a simple collaboration tool, which allows you to share a notebook with multiple people in your team, making it a very powerful use of its functionality. It does pose some complications if you have sensitive content that you don't want to share with the whole team, as you can only share the full notebook, not just the individual page. But you can password protect each section of the notebook if needed though. Otherwise, consider having one notebook for each direct report.

So, strategy one is having a central place to capture discussion items. Strategy two is making that a shared collaboration space for you and your reports. Strategy three is linking emails and other digital information to this notebook. As I mention earlier in this chapter, you can easily send an email from your inbox to a OneNote notebook so you have the relevant information to discuss at your fingertips. Look for the 'Send to OneNote' button in the Ribbon Toolbar in your Inbox. It is very easy to use and a very powerful tool for 1:1 discussions.

But for strategies like this to work, you *all* need to buy into it as a team. One leader I worked with was so excited about the possibilities, she set up her notebooks straight away. The next time I caught up with her she was frustrated. She was fully committed, but found her direct reports had their own preferences. Mary liked to use her Moleskine, Brad used EverNote and Matt was happy to give it a go, but kept forgetting to add his discussion items to the list. You get the picture.

I took a very strong position on this. In this case, personal preferences were getting in the way of group productivity.

I told her that she should set an expectation for the team to adopt this tool and this strategy because it made sense, and with a little effort, would benefit all of them. After this they got on board and were all more productive as a result.

Coach your team to make your life easier

Coaching people to make your life easier sounds incredibly gratuitous and selfish, but it isn't, I assure you. This concept fits squarely into the win/win box. As a leader, if you make it easy for me, I can move things forward more quickly for you. You need to make it as easy as possible for me to turn things around, as my schedule is full, my inbox is overflowing and I don't have a lot of time.

Barack Obama was known for how he dealt with memos when in office. He asked for every memo to fit onto a single A4 page and to have three boxes printed at the foot of the page: 'yes', 'no' and 'let's discuss'. This made it easier for him to quickly read the memo and make a decision.

I worked with an IT director once who had a huge pile of reports spread all over her desk in neat piles. When I asked her what they were, she told me they were proposals from her team for projects they wanted her approval on. The problem was, each one was at least 40 pages long, and she did not have time to read them all. So they sat there for months. My advice? Insist that every proposal have a covering executive summary that could be read in a few minutes to help her to quickly filter the wheat from the chaff. She could then read deeper into the few that warranted it when she needed to.

I also recommend getting your direct team to practice writing one-minute emails, that is, emails you can read in less than one minute. You don't have time to wade through complex, long-winded emails when a short, succinct email would do a more effective job.

These are all strategies that help busy executives keep things moving. But all too often, our teams dive into detail, writing stream of consciousness emails that take us minutes, if not hours, to decipher. It may take a little longer for them to craft a well-written, succinct communication, but the win is you are more likely to respond quickly if you don't have to devote too much of your bandwidth to it.

Share the decision workload

An evolution of this idea is how you and your team can share the decision workload. I am sure they are constantly asking you for decisions, and chasing you on your response. What is often needed to speed this process up is a sharing of the decision workload, where you both agree to doing a piece of the work to reach a speedy but solid decision.

The more clearly and succinctly they can describe the situation and their recommendation to you, the easier it is for you to deliberate and decide. But if they are in the habit of presenting you with problems rather than solutions, they are delegating the work to you to assess the situation, make recommendations to yourself, then deliberate on the best course of action before deciding. How often do you put off what should be a straightforward decision because you feel you don't have the time or the bandwidth to get your head around the detail? How often are you either presented with no useful detail or so much detail that it is too much work to get across it? Get your team to do their part of the work, and you can focus on yours.

Your team should own steps one and two in figure 5.2. They need to be able to succinctly describe the situation, and then make a recommendation to you. This could be a proposed

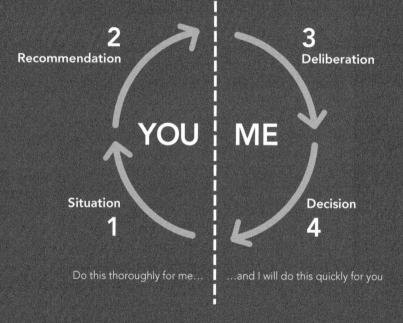

Figure 5.2: Sharing the decision workload

course of action for approval, or two or three suggested options. You can then own steps three and four. You deliberate on the information and recommendations they have provided, and then make and communicate a decision.

Again, this is a great coaching moment, and most team members are responsive to frameworks like this. They make sense, but many people have just never thought about the mechanics of how they work before, so they may never have noticed how their behaviours can slow things down and create more work for others.

● ● ●

In the next chapter, we will look at delegation strategies that are relevant to your direct reports as well as the wider team. There may be lessons you should learn yourself, and certainly there will be lessons that you will want to coach your direct reports on.

Reflections and intentions

- Is your EA active or passive? What do you need to help them step up to the next level?

- Do you need to be more faithful to your regular catch-up with your EA?

- Do you want to be self-driven or chauffeur-driven with your calendar or inbox?

- Do your direct reports make it easy for you to make decisions for them?

- Think about your preferred productivity style (Organiser, Energiser, Analyser). How does your style impact on how you work with your EA and direct reports?

CHAPTER 6
Delegate early and well

Delegation, in the corporate work context, is the act of assigning the responsibility of a task or a project to someone else. It is a crucial tool in a leader's kitbag, and one, unfortunately, not always used as often as it should be or with enough attention to quality.

In most teams, work is often created by the leader, or will flow through the leader to their team. Of course, this is not always the case, and in the most effective teams, work will flow below the level of the leader and not need to involve them at all. But when issues arise, or opportunities pop up, or a course of action is decided upon, it may fall to the leader to decide who they delegate the execution of the work to, and to ensure that it is done in a timely way to the right level of quality.

This is often not as easy as it sounds, as you are busy, they are busy, and this new piece of work is probably competing with many other priorities and deadlines. But if done in the right way, delegation is the key to the effective progression of work in a high-performance team.

When should you delegate?

Q: When should we delegate?

A: Whenever the work is a better use of someone else's time or skillset.

One of the main reasons why leaders and managers may not delegate as much as they should is a need for control. They might not see it that way, and often tell themselves stories about why they are not delegating the work: 'My team is already overloaded'; 'It would be quicker to just do it myself'; 'They won't do it right as they don't have my experience'. These stories that we tell ourselves are just us getting in our way.

The only story that is true and worth telling is that every time you, as a leader, are working below the line, you are not working above the line. The opportunity cost for you if you do not delegate the right work to others is massive. There is always something more valuable that you are not doing if you hold on to below the line work. So, the key is to delegate anything that requires action, but you consider below the line for you. The work you did in chapter 4 should help you to identify what is worth delegating.

Every time you, as a leader, are working below the line, you are not working above the line. The opportunity cost for you if you do not delegate the right work to others is massive.

One of the leaps I needed to make as I grew my business and my team was learning to let go of this work, no exceptions. I am now pretty ruthless at delegating, and delegating early, but for a number of years, I would hold on to way too much. When I started to work with the above the line/below the line framework we cover in chapter 4, I started to become more and more ruthless about the things that were dragging me below the line. There was a period where I was the leader, but I was working harder than everyone around me. Now, working hard or working long hours is a choice we make, and is fine if we are doing the right work. But I found myself working harder to do my work as well as other people's work. This was not *their* fault, it was mine. I needed to learn to delegate consistently, efficiently and in a timely way.

A second consideration in relation to 'when' you should delegate, is to consider if you tend to delegate early enough. It is easy to procrastinate over requests that come to you that should be delegated. You hold on for too long, and suddenly you are in a position where it is too late to delegate and you have to do it yourself. It may have been an email in your inbox that you should have been more decisive about, and now a week later they are chasing you and delegation is not an option. Or it may be a project that was not urgent a month ago, but now the deadline is looming, and you are going to have to get more involved than you should. Not delegating early enough may also be creating reactive urgency that was avoidable for your team. Remember, first, do no harm!

How should you delegate?

When you do delegate, it is important to delegate in a clear and purposeful way. When we are busy there can be a tendency to flick the work on without enough thought or guidance, which just leads to frustration for the person you're delegating to, and of course, you, if you don't get the results you expected. Delegating work is like passing the baton in a relay race: you both need to be ready, both need to understand the process at play, and you both have some responsibility in the effective transfer of the work. The passing over of the baton needs to be clean, otherwise the race is lost.

Effective delegations are:

- *considered*, with thought going into the purpose of the work, who the best person to delegate to might be, and what actually needs to be delivered and to what level of quality

- *clear*, with a conversation that specifies the work and expectations, and allows for negotiation and clarification by the person being delegated to

- *timely*, delegated early enough to allow the person being delegated to to plan effectively.

Before I started my own business, I worked for a global time management training company. This was in the 1990s, when paper diary systems were the go-to productivity tool. I remember there was a delegation tool that came as a part of the diary system, and it was really useful. It was a simple one-page delegation form, which required the delegator to fill out a full description of what was being delegated, what the expected outcomes should be, when it was expected by and what the agreed communication plan was to discuss progress on the delegation. It was nothing complicated, but it ensured some rigour around the delegation. Tools like this have fallen by the wayside as we have shifted to email and technology to manage our work, but maybe we would benefit from going back to old-school tools that were effective in these cases. Maybe you could create similar templates in your electronic tools to enforce some rigour around delegations. A tool such as OneNote could be perfect for this as it allows page templates to be created easily.

Whatever tool you use, the clarity of the delegation is the most important factor, and that requires leaders to make the time to delegate well.

Get specific with your delegations

Being specific can help when it comes to clarity. When we are not specific about what we want, people may deliver us things that we don't want. A good example of this was the day my wife delegated something to me but, unfortunately, did not get the result she wanted. She told me the name of a laundry softener (Fluffy, to be exact), and asked me to buy some at the shops. She even sent me a picture of the label to be sure I got the right one. I made a note of this on my phone, so I did not forget on my way home from the office.

I bought the bottle of Fluffy as requested — such a well organised partner, I thought to myself! When I got home, it turned out that I got the wrong one. Grrr! I got the right brand, but I bought the large bottle that won't fit in the laundry cupboard, not the small one she had wanted. Not the end of the world, but I thought this was a great lesson in delegation. *If you want a specific result, get specific when you delegate!*

Vera's assumption was that, by showing me the label, I would buy that exact bottle. But without a qualifying statement about being sure to buy the small one, my assumption was that she wanted that brand, but had no strong opinion about size or any other measurement. Nobody was really in the wrong here, we were just both busy and trying to get this done in the cracks. This is when mistakes happen, and work is wasted or needs to be redone.

In the workplace, this sort of miscommunication happens a lot. We delegate work to others and assume that their thinking is the same as ours. But when we work in complex teams, with a diverse range of personalities and skillsets, our thinking is often very different. We need to be careful not to make assumptions, and to take time to think through what we specifically want before we delegate.

Of course, if you do not need a very specific result, and are happy to leave it up to your team member to make decisions about the detail, then delegate the general outcome you want. But if you want a specific outcome, to a specific level of quality, then delegate specifically. This may take more time and effort, but in the long run, time is saved for both of you. Please don't feel that I am suggesting that you can't let your team think for themselves, or that you have to spell everything out in minute detail. Just don't be vague and then cranky if you don't get exactly what you expected.

Tell them what not to do

I love to build Ikea furniture. No joke, I love it. It is like Lego for me, a creative exercise with step-by-step instructions. Recently, during one of my building projects, I got myself into a bit of trouble. About halfway into building a set of shelves, I ran into a dead end. The part I needed to put on next would not fit. I went back to the instructions, retraced my steps, and low and behold, I had not followed the instructions carefully enough.

A few steps before, the instructions clearly showed how to put on one of the shelving brackets, and it clearly showed what *not* to do. *Do not put on the bracket with the holes on the top.* Make sure the holes line up on the bottom, the instructions said. This turned out to be my problem. Further down the track I could not fit the shelf because the holes were in the wrong position. I had to take it all apart again and redo the build the right way.

Even though I messed up, I believe that Ikea instructions are really good at helping the builder to avoid mistakes like this. They clearly show you what to do, and what *not* to do. The problem was, in my enthusiasm, and maybe arrogant self-confidence, I did not read the instructions fully.

When we delegate work, it's also a good idea to tell people what *not* to do. Ikea know the common mistakes people make when building their products that just lead to frustration and rework, so they communicate them up front. With your experience, you may also know the common mistakes the people you delegate to could make. It's worth taking the time to think through what it is you want them to deliver. Include with this any relevant insights into the traps they should try to avoid when doing the work. Of course, be sure you take their experience into account, as you don't want to teach your team how to suck eggs.

A lot of time and energy is wasted on rework and on fixing mistakes, often because work was not delegated properly in the first place. There is an old saying: 'If it is worth doing, it is worth doing well.' We could add to that with: 'If it is worth delegating, it is worth delegating well.'

Effective delegation matrix

In *Smart Work* I unpacked a delegation framework that considered the risk or complexity of the task, and the experience of the person being delegated to, and then prescribed some options for how hands-on or hands-off you should be in the delegation. Even if you are familiar with this framework, I think it is worth discussing again here to examine some nuances that might help you think more thoroughly about your delegations. Figure 6.1 (overleaf) is an evolution of the delegation framework from *Smart Work*.

In the scenarios that follow, what I mean by risk is the impact that the job being done incorrectly or delivered late would have for you, your team or the organisation. As a leader, you may need to use your judgement of the level of risk with each delegation.

Be hands-off and get out of their way

In this scenario, you are dealing with team members who have experience and whom you trust and the risk is low. Delegate clearly, but then take a hands-off approach and *get out of their way*. In fact, in this scenario, you may not even need to have a conversation about this; it could be an email with the clear direction that you trust them to be able to work out the best course of action. If it is low risk, you probably don't even need a status report on progress or completion; trust that it will be done unless there are other factors at play.

Be hands-on and partner with them

In a situation where you have no choice but to delegate something that carries higher risk, and you are not totally comfortable with their level of experience, you need to be hands-on and make the time to *partner with them* to achieve the outcome. This is a part of your role as a leader, and a 'moment of impact' that will increase their experience quickly. But you need to be the safety net to make sure that, if anything goes off the rails, you can step in to catch it. A very clear, face-to-face delegation is required here, with lots of agreed check-ins and progress reports. You may even do some of the work yourself, but have them observe you to understand how you handle it. This is

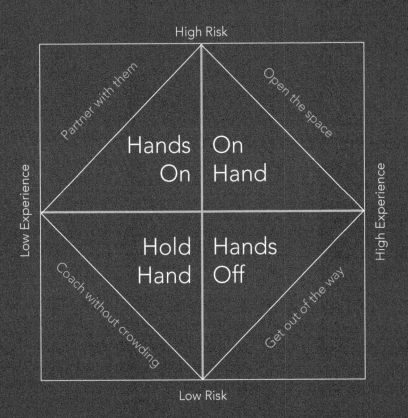

Figure 6.1: The delegation matrix

such a great learning opportunity, and I worry that sometimes we are too busy to make the time for these opportunities.

Hold their hand and coach without crowding

When your team member has limited experience, but the task is low risk, you have more leeway to let them at it themselves, knowing they may not get it perfect the first time. You should hold their hand and *coach them without crowding them*. You might ask them to bring their progress to you at regular intervals so you can provide coaching without doing the work for them. It's like taking the training wheels off a child's bike. You then run with them, holding the saddle until they are up and going. You then let go, and off they go. They might not even realise that you are no longer holding them, but hopefully they realise that they can do it, and that you are still running alongside them if they have a wobble.

Be on-hand and open the space

Finally, if your team member is experienced, but there is risk involved with the task, you need to be on-hand, available to provide input if and when it is needed. But you need to step back and *open the space* for them to do the work their way, and let them use you as a trusted advisor, rather than a micro-managing boss. You need to be available for questions or issues that arise, which we will talk about more in chapter 7.

A good leader delegates as much as possible, getting lots of plates spinning at once. These plates may need the odd booster spin from you, but if you are nimble and have good systems in place, you should be able to apply minimal touches to keep everything moving nicely.

Cc and delegation

Within the context of the delegation matrix framework, it might be worth thinking about the role of Cc in your emails when it comes to delegation. This is far from the only way that Cc traffic builds up between a team and their leader, but it is a contributor to the volume of email that a leader receives. Some clear direction about Cc expectations when delegating work can reduce unnecessary emails.

Here is an example of the unnecessary use of Cc in a delegation. I received an email from a manager in a client company, requesting information on our productivity training program for his team. He let me know that his boss had completed the training in the past, and had suggested that the manager reach out to me to organise the same training for his direct team.

I noticed his boss leader was copied into this email. It got me thinking about why this would be. Given the seniority of the manager sending me the email (not quite a senior executive, but senior enough to lead his own team), why would his even more senior manager need to be copied on this communication?

The Cc function has many purposes, not all of them productive. Essentially, Cc is used as a way of maintaining oversight and control. The need for this control can be driven by the Cc recipient or can be driven by the sender. Either way, in this case, the Cc seemed unnecessary to me. The task in question, to enquire about pricing for a training program, should have been delegated without the need for oversight. Maybe it was, but the manager involved had a habit of assuming that his manager needed to be looped in on everything. I don't know the answer in this specific case, but can imagine one of the following circumstances leading to the Cc.

- The divisional leader had specifically requested to be copied, even though there was little need.

- The divisional leader had a general policy that he be copied in on any emails from his reporting managers.

- The manager sending the email assumed that his boss wanted to be copied in.

- The manager wanted his boss to see he was doing the work.

- The manager was copying his boss as a way of ensuring that I responded promptly to the email.

- The manager just did not think.

I do not believe that any of these scenarios are productive. It was only one email, but multiply that across hundreds of emails each week, and it creates a lot of noise for the divisional leader. It also begins to pollute the team culture as others see this behaviour and copy it, just to cover themselves.

Using the delegation matrix outlined on page 130, you can map the following Cc directions to each quadrant.

- **Hands-off:** No need to copy me at all, I trust your work and your judgement.

- **Hands-on:** Cc me on all communications about this task, so I can jump in and help if I believe it is needed.

- **Hold-hand:** Use your judgement and Cc me or check with me if you are unsure.

- **On-hand:** Use your own judgement.

Sometimes, without clear direction on stuff like this, our team takes one of two positions. They over-copy us and bombard us with unnecessary emails, or they under-copy us and expose us when we should have been across an issue or topic. It is impossible to always get it right, but the more you coach your team to be purposeful in keeping you in the loop on the right things, the better it will be for all involved.

Track your delegations

One of the possible reasons you may not delegate as much as you should is that you are worried that you will lose track of the work, and therefore lose control. In fact, I would say control issues are at the heart of the problem of not delegating enough.

As I discussed in chapter 3 with deep and wide focus, it is challenging enough to keep track of everything that we need to do ourselves, let along track everything that our team is doing on our behalf. Of course, not everything needs tracking, and many things can be delegated with trust and an expectation that it will be done. But with less-experienced team members, or with work that carries more risk or a need for you to stay aware of the progress of the work, it is worth tracking.

Once a task or project has been delegated, and I decide it is worth tracking, I use one of a number of strategies. Sometimes it will suffice to capture it as a discussion point in our 1:1 list discussion list in OneNote, so I remember to check in on progress in our next catch-up.

If it is more time-sensitive than that, say a report that I need before a key meeting, I will schedule a task a few days ahead of the meeting to trigger a reminder for myself that they were meant to get back to me with the work in question. I often label this task as a 'due from others', so it shows up in this format:

Due: Tony re FAQ questions draft list

This is often all I need to track the progress, and not lose sight of it amongst all of the other things that are happening in my busy mind.

Sometimes sharing this work in a collaboration platform that is visible to both you and your team is a better option. Most teams now have access to simple electronic project or Kanban boards in tools like MS Teams or Jira that allow us to create a task, assign it to the appropriate person and keep track of the status of the work. A board like this can be used for project work, but you can also set up a team board, with the board organised by 'assigned' so that you get a column for each person in your team, with each column containing the active delegated tasks for each person. Figure 6.2 shows an example of a team board in MS Planner.

Figure 6.2: An electronic project board

Successful tracking of delegated work requires two ingredients:

- *delegators* who consistently capture what needs to be tracked, and set clear expectations around deadlines

- *delegates* who take ownership of delivering on time, and put their hand up if that is not possible by updating any shared delegation tools with progress details.

Set clear expectations about the updating of the status of work with your team, but don't make their life a misery with so much updating and admin that they can't get their work done. Choose what to track wisely, but trust that they will do what you ask by the deadline as much as you can.

● ● ●

Your ability to pass the baton in the delegation relay, and then support the other runners in the team, can make or break productive delegation. Of course, when you do delegate work, there will be times when your team needs to check things with you, to run things past you, to get approval or to get direction. That means you need to be available and responsive to them. That's what we will discuss in the next chapter. But first, time to reflect.

Reflections and intentions

- Do you delegate enough 'below the line' work?

- Do you pass the baton as cleanly as you should when delegating work?

- How do you track what has been delegated to whom?

- What conversations could you have with your team to improve the delegation process between you?

- Think about your preferred productivity style (Organiser, Energiser, Analyser). How does your style impact how you delegate to your team members, especially if they have a different style to you?

CHAPTER 7

Be responsive, not reactive

You may think like to think of yourself as a highly responsive leader, but your team may disagree. I was working with an insurance company senior executive, his EA and his operations manager to boost the productivity of the three of them as a unit. The coaching sessions were well received, and the leader was open to new ways of working to get on top of a huge role with many moving parts. Everyone was positive and keen to develop a more productive way of working.

In one of the coaching sessions, the leader had to leave 15 minutes early because of an unavoidable meeting clash. The remaining three of us decided to stay on to agree to an action plan. While the leader's team was very positive about how the leader worked with them when he was in the room, as soon as the door closed, what was really happening came out, loud and clear!

It turned out the leader, in the eyes of the two people that he worked most closely with, was extremely reactive, and this was making their life hell. He was spending way too much time in meetings that he really did not need to attend, was rarely available to his direct reports, was constantly dropping urgent last-minute requests on everyone, and was usually catching up on emails at 11 pm at night, creating a feeling that they should all be responding at that time.

As a leader, you must be responsive, not reactive. This means you deal with things in a timely way, setting the tone for proactivity within your team. You avoid creating reactive dramas for your team, but rather work as proactively as possible, coaching others to do likewise. When work is truly urgent, you deal with it appropriately, but you always question urgency and expect urgent work to be the exception, not the rule.

You also try to keep the work flowing for your team by staying in control of your inbox, and you make sure you have availability if you're needed to deal with urgent issues or decisions. You work hard to avoid being the bottleneck for workflow in your team, and you have reasonable expectations about deadlines, being willing to push back and negotiate with the business if your team is being hammered by unreasonable deadlines.

Which image represents your way of working? Are you like the insurance company leader or a more responsive and available leader? Working responsively and proactively is challenging, especially in workplaces that thrive on urgency and reactivity. But it is one of the most critical skills for any leader who aims to work at the elite level of productivity. Just like a first responder to an accident scene is trained to walk in calmly and slowly, you need to go about your work in a calm and measured way. You need to set the example for others, and you need to make sure you are not the one creating productivity friction for others because of your reactive work style. And, of course, you will personally benefit from a more proactive work style, as you will experience less unnecessary stress.

In my book *Urgent!*, I described the difference between reactivity and responsiveness as 'knee-jerk' versus 'measured'. When we are reactive, there is an instinctive reaction rather than a thought-through response to the situation. You might think, 'What's the problem with that?' As a leader, you may feel like you have honed your instincts and are more agile because of your fast responses. But it is rarely the case that reactivity creates a good outcome for you or the people around you. It just escalates the stress, and affects the ability of people to focus on what is truly important in their roles. When you are reactive as a leader, you feed a culture of urgency that permeates many modern organisations, where the only prioritisation lens people examine work through is the urgency lens. Many organisations talk the talk about enabling their people to work on the important work, but they don't walk the walk. They foster reactive cultures where urgency is expected, and reactivity rewarded. Of course, if things are truly urgent, then *act immediately* by all means. But most of the time you should be in a position as a leader to *respond appropriately*, rather than having a knee-jerk reaction.

As an extension of this, we would aim to move beyond reacting and responding to the more planned end of the reactive/proactive spectrum in figure 7.1 (overleaf). Your role should be firmly focused on more than reacting to the day-to-day issues in the business; it should also be focused on being predictive, and trying to anticipate issues or opportunities coming down the track. When we *anticipate early*, we reduce the risk of problems arising in the first place, and we can put contingency plans in place if issues do arise.

The most impactful place on the reactive/proactive spectrum is working proactively by planning thoroughly. Leaders who create the space in their schedule to plan ahead are the ones

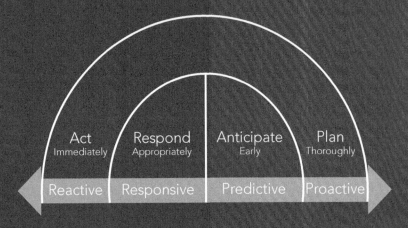

Figure 7.1: Reactive/proactive spectrum

who have the most impact. The Organisers among us love to hear this, as it fits with our world view. The Energisers and Analysers can struggle with this, as planning ahead is not always their strong suit. But planning at the individual level, at the team level and at the organisational level is crucial, and can make you and your team much more proactive and less reactive.

I don't believe that we need to be reactive to be productive. I don't believe we need to move at 1000 miles an hour all of the time, striving to get more and more done, faster and faster. So, let's have a look at some strategies to help you work more responsively with your team, and more proactively in general, starting with your approach to your inbox and email.

Responsiveness to email

Most leaders would say that email is not the most critical thing they deal with in their role, but it still causes a measure of angst, and makes them feel guilty when they are not on top of it all. How we deal with emails as a leader is also on show for others, and becomes a part of our leadership brand. My biggest concern with how you manage your email is related to your team and your other key stakeholders. They are the ones who suffer if you are not responsive to the actions in your inbox.

I worked with one leader in a workshop who shared an, unfortunately, common approach to email. Unless the email was from his boss, one of his senior peers or a key team member, he basically ignored it. He said that they would follow up if it was important, and when they chased him three times, he might consider taking notice. I questioned why he took that approach, and he replied that he simply got too many emails each day to respond to them all. From memory, he was receiving in excess of 200 emails per day.

Now while, on one level, I agree that he is getting too many emails to respond to them all, I disagree with his approach. This executive was disadvantaging other people who had legitimate needs, because he had not taken ownership of his email volume. He had become a victim of email noise, and his response was to abdicate responsibility for his email unless it was from one of the key people in his world. This feels like a knee-jerk reaction to me, and I know there is a more effective approach that would better serve both the executive and his team and colleagues. Managing people's expectations is far more effective than ignoring emails.

In my early twenties, I was always impressed by some of the bartenders in my local pub in Dublin. On a Friday or Saturday night the pub would be heaving with people, and the 15 m-long bar could be six-deep with merry punters trying to order drinks. An inexperienced bartender would keep their head down and just try to serve the person right in front of them. They would avoid eye contact at all costs, with the mindset of 'if I see you, I must serve you'. When the punters were ignored like this, they got a little feral and tried desperately to get to the front of the crowd to get noticed. It was each one for themselves, and much pushing and jostling would ensue!

But there were a few bartenders who really knew their stuff. Rather than look down to avoid eye contact, they looked up and caught the eye of the people in the queue. And with a simple nod, you knew you were on their radar. They did not serve you next, but you knew they would get to you in a fair and timely way. I reckon I would happily wait ten minutes after getting the nod without becoming frustrated.

This is a great example of professional people working under pressure, but managing expectations really well. In our corporate workplaces, we can take a lesson from this. Our brand is on show all the time, and people will enjoy working with you if they can trust you. They will be more forgiving and open to negotiation if you manage their expectations well.

To build trust through responsiveness, take ownership of the volume of emails that you receive. But strategies in place to reduce the volume of noise that breaks through, and be responsive to the requests that come from your team, your peers, other stakeholders and clients. Taking a position that you will not bother to respond to certain emails until they chase you several times is a selfish position that sends a terrible message to others.

Email overwhelm kills your responsiveness

The key issue that most leaders are facing in respect to responsiveness is simply email overwhelm. Too many emails, and too little time to keep across them. I believe there are three core reasons why leaders can become overwhelmed by email (see figure 7.2, overleaf).

- They are *inundated* with emails and email noise, getting overwhelmed by the sheer volume and the number of emails.

- They are *inconsistent* with the time they devote to email processing, trying to fit it into the cracks rather than seeing email processing as a legitimate maintenance activity that deserves dedicated time and attention.

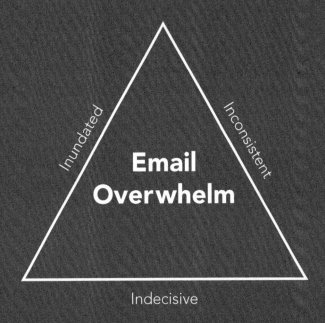

Figure 7.2: Causes of email overwhelm

- When they do look at their inbox, they are *indecisive* about what to do with emails, and end up leaving them to pile up, a messy jumble of read and unread, flagged and unflagged, relevant and irrelevant.

Each of these causes of email overwhelm are easily addressed and can lead to you getting in control of your inbox. And the surprising thing is that you will actually spend less time on email if you get in control of it. You do not need to spend hours per day clearing emails, which to me would be 'below the line' work for you. Instead, you will ruthlessly and efficiently make decisions and move things forward for yourself and others.

What to do if you are inundated with email

If you are in the situation where you get hundreds of emails each day, don't feel bad if you cannot stay on top of the deluge. No one could stay on top of that many messages each day. It's funny that we are even expected to. My father, in his role as a senior finance leader, used to keep a memo pad on his desk. I distinctly remember going into his office as a kid and playing with the carbon paper that sat between the sheets of paper. My recollection is there were six sheets of carbon paper that his assistant placed between the first six pages in the notepad each morning. If my father wrote a memo to his leadership team, the memo was copied onto the six pages, and put in each manager's pigeonhole for them to review. This was the 1970s, before email, and seems to me like it was an easier volume of information to manage than what we have to deal with today.

The first thing we need to do is get in control of the email noise. This involves taking ownership of what is coming into your inbox, and taking action to reduce the noise. For me, email noise is anything I receive that does not add value to me or my role, so I apply the following strategies to either delete the noise altogether or move it to another place where I can deal with it when I have the time.

- As discussed on page 112, I move emails I am Cc'd on to a Cc folder to review if and when I need to. I work on the assumption that there are no actions for me in a Cc, and that should be your expectation too. I do review this folder, usually every couple of days when I have a bit of space, and this reduces a lot of noise in my inbox, and allows me to focus on what is sent directly to me when processing emails. Coaching your team to use Cc in this way sets expectations, but also lets them know you have oversight of what is going on.

- I use the 'Focused' inbox function in MS Outlook to divert less-essential emails, like newsletters and marketing emails into an 'Other' tab. Once you have turned this feature on (it's likely a default setting in your organisation), you can then right-click on any email to choose whether it appears in your 'Focused' tab or 'Other' tab in the future. This, again, reduces so much noise for me, and allows me to focus more on what is important in my inbox. I also completely delete the emails in my 'Other' tab each day.

- I use rules to move informative emails, like approvals or reading, to a batching folder, again, so I can review them when I have time.

- I have my EA cull non-critical emails or things that she can deal with if I am in training or travelling, and not getting to my inbox as often as I usually would.

- I have had conversations with my team about when I need to be copied in on emails, and on the cautious use of 'reply all' to minimise email noise generated by them.

- I have coached my team to write emails in a way that makes it easy for me to quickly understand and respond to. These are clear, concise emails with a summary if needed, and actions highlighted. This is a win/win, as my email burden is lighter, and they get a response more quickly.

Email noise is a reality of our modern, email-driven workplace. But it is manageable if we actively take steps to manage it. When you reduce the noise, it is much easier to be responsive to the signal. I see *signal* as the emails that need my attention, and *noise* as emails that get in the way and obscure the signal. Noise reduction is an ongoing task, and we need to keep working on the noise levels, but if I take action the moment I spot emails coming in that I really should not be receiving, then it's not an arduous task. Just as pulling out weeds in the garden when you spot them means you don't have to spend all weekend weeding the garden every few months.

What to do if you are inconsistent with email processing

Like it or not, email requires our time, energy and focus. How you feel about that may depend on whether you identify with being an Organiser, an Energiser or an Analyser. Organisers are more likely to invest the time to keep their inbox down to a manageable number of emails awaiting their attention. That is a bit of a generalisation, but mostly true, I suspect. Energisers may be more likely to let their emails build up and then they attack them in a frenzy of energy and activity. Again, a generalisation, but not inaccurate in many cases. Analysers may ignore emails when they are deeply focused, but like to stay across it when they are not.

Email requires time, but it should not consume too much of our time. We should invest enough time in email to keep things moving. Now, if you have put the right strategies in place to reduce the noise, what is left in your inbox that requires a decision from you should be a more manageable number, allowing you to process emails a couple of times each day. But if you don't invest this time to properly focus on email, if you try to just do it in the cracks between meetings, it will defeat you.

I personally check my email about once per hour. I have turned off all email alerts so I don't get distracted by email, but I do connect with my inbox regularly to see if anything needs my urgent attention, or can be moved on quickly with a response. These hourly checks are usually five-minute checks, after which I get back to my other priorities.

But twice per day I will properly process emails. I devote 30 to 45 minutes to making decisions about the emails in my inbox. Once I have dealt with an email, I will either delete it or file it, and I treat my inbox purely as a delivery dock for new work coming in, not a storeroom for old messages.

I talked earlier about the balance between your time in meetings and time protected for other work. I also protect time in my day to process emails, and see it as a necessary piece of maintenance. One of my senior clients calls his similar approach to inbox management 'basic hygiene'. He devotes time each day to stay on top of his email just like he devotes time each day to showering and brushing his teeth. I like that idea.

Even if I spend 45 minutes in the morning on email, and another 30 minutes in the late afternoon, and five minutes per hour outside of those times, I reckon I am investing 1.5 to two hours on email per day. I reckon this is far less than the average Australian worker spends on email each day.

One of my senior clients calls his similar approach to inbox management as 'basic hygiene'. He devotes time each day to stay on top of his email just like he devotes time each day to showering and brushing his teeth.

What to do if you are indecisive about emails

The final key to staying on top of email is *decisiveness*. Because we are regularly inundated and overwhelmed by emails, and because we are often receiving poorly written emails that are hard to decipher, we can sometimes look at an email, feel it is too hard for right now and procrastinate. The risk is that, as more emails pile on top, the list of things needing our attention grows. And because our inbox is not a very effective action management system, we fall behind on responses, and end up with people chasing us, forcing you into a reactive corner.

One of my clients told me about an email that had been stuck in his inbox for over a month. It had been sent to him from his boss, but while the task itself was worthy, it was not business critical, so he left it in his inbox, and started to procrastinate. Over the ensuing month, he felt more and more guilty about this task sitting incomplete in his inbox. When we talked about it, my advice was that what he needed to do to be more decisive with these types of emails was to focus less on *completion*, and more on *traction*. In his mind, he felt that he should devote the time to completing that piece of work, but knew it was not his top priority. In my mind, he just needed to get some traction and get it started. Could he have flicked it on to his EA to set up a meeting? Could he have reached out to the stakeholder involved and given them a heads up that it was on his radar, but he would not get to it for a few weeks? All it needed was a decision and some traction.

In *Smart Work* I outlined an approach to email that has decisiveness at its heart. First of all, treat your inbox as a delivery dock, not a filing system and not a to-do list. If an email signals you need to do something, whether that be respond to it or do an action within the email, either do it and file or delete the email, or schedule it in your calendar or task list for future action. MS Outlook and Gmail both allow you to convert emails into tasks or calendar entries. Your inbox was never designed to manage actions, but your task list and calendar are designed for that very purpose. These tools allow you to manage your time around the action, and add some level of priority to the activity. Moving an email out of your inbox and scheduling it into your task list for another time is *intentional*. Leaving an email in your inbox for later is procrastination.

As mentioned on page 111, there are four things you can with any email: you can *dump it, divert it, decide when* to deal with it, or you can do it now. The elite approach to your inbox is to be ruthless in this decision making. Force yourself to make quick, action oriented decisions about as many emails as you can. Of course, some require more thought and reflection, but scheduling time for that is also a decision.

Leaders who take this decisive approach to emails can easily maintain an inbox with minimal emails in it, and even achieve an empty inbox weekly. Basic hygiene!

Our inbox, and how full or empty it is, or how messy or organised it is, is the sum of the choices we make. Just like a teenager's messy room is the sum of the choices they make about their clothes and possessions, if we have a messy inbox, we cannot place the blame anywhere but at our own feet. If we allow too much noise in, that is our problem. If we have constructed a complicated filing system of 87 folders, that is our problem. If we fail to invest time to process email each day, that is our problem. So let's not be victims here, but be responsible email users and leaders.

Make yourself more available

Responsiveness is not a concept solely restricted to email management. Being responsive to the needs of your team, peers and stakeholders requires a certain amount of your time, energy and focus to be available as needed. It can be frustrating for others if you are never available because of your compressed meeting schedule.

One of my clients told me the story of how, when he returned to his team's workspace in between his endless meetings, he would get mobbed by people needing his attention. He said that people would follow him into the toilet until he politely but firmly told them to give him a minute! But you can understand their need, and the feeling that if they don't speak to him now, it might be days before they get to see him again.

As a leader, availability is one of your superpowers, just like the CEO on page 92 who was available to meet with one of his team that week, compared with the manager involved not being free for a month. That is powerful, and allows for moments of impact where you can unlock something, keep the work flowing or inspire someone in that moment of availability.

The first strategy to make yourself more available is to balance your schedule so you are not spending too much of your time in meetings (which is why chapter 2 on balance is so important). For me, the 50 per cent of my time that I protect for work outside of meetings is used to work on my priorities, to process emails, to plan and prepare, and to be available to my team and clients as things come up.

A few of my senior clients like to schedule advertised drop-in times for their team each week. They allocate two or three one-hour slots in the week where they base themselves in a meeting room, and if any of the team need ten minutes with them, they know where to find them and get their full attention. This is great if you have more formal weekly catch-ups with your team, and you want to move to a bi-weekly or monthly cycle, as they always know they can get you in between if needed. This can be done in a meeting room if you are in the office, or through a tool like MS Teams or Zoom if working remotely.

The secret to a strategy like this working is to be very clear about the ground rules. Just because you may be available for the advertised hour on Wednesday afternoon, does not mean that they can hog the whole hour. Be clear that this time is for focused discussions that should take no more than ten minutes. Also ensure that they come focused and prepared, otherwise they will be wasting your precious time.

My client who had people following him to the toilet adopted these strategies, and went from feedback surveys saying that he was rarely available to him becoming one of the most available senior managers in the group. His team loved that he was so available to them.

The marshmallow choice

When it comes to being available, one of the challenges you probably face on a regular basis is people wanting to meet with you urgently, throwing your day or week into disruption as you try to squeeze them in at the last minute. This is probably not just your team, but peers and stakeholders as well. Of course, urgency will always play a part in our work, and is unavoidable sometimes, but as we have discussed in chapter 2, work is often not as urgent as people make it out to be.

A good way to deal with this sort of disruption is to give people what I call the marshmallow choice. One of the most famous psychological tests ever conducted was created by Walter Mischel in the 1960s. It examined the concept of delayed gratification, and the level of self-control demonstrated by children. In short, the children were given a simple choice related to a marshmallow placed on the table in front of them. The person running the experiment told them that they were going to leave the room for a few minutes. If the child did not eat the marshmallow, they would get two when the adult came back.

Now, I believe in the old adage that a bird in the hand is worth two in the bush. I would have gone for the marshmallow I had rather than wait. But some kids did wait. The original experiment showed that, when they interviewed the children a few years later, the ones who chose to delay their gratification in the test had achieved a greater level of academic achievement in later life. Subsequent studies have thrown up some more nuanced results, but it's a fascinating study nonetheless.

This can be used as a great strategy to reduce the negative impact of urgent meeting pressures on your schedule, and to make others value your availability more. The next time somebody comes to you or your EA asking to see you urgently to discuss an issue, give them a choice: 'I can give you ten minutes tomorrow, or 30 minutes next week.'

People need to value your time, not take it for granted. And this is a reasonable choice. We can get together tomorrow in a short but focused way to have a quick discussion, or we can deal with it in more detail next week. You are asking them which is the more valuable option for them. They get to choose, so this makes them feel that they have some power in the situation.

When people realise that they cannot just take your time in a blasé fashion, they become more mindful about what is really necessary in the situation.

The key to this strategy working well is actually having some spare capacity in your schedule for the ten minutes. Make sure your schedule is not so compressed that you cannot offer the single marshmallow. And of course, there needs to be a clear expectation that ten minutes is ten minutes, and people need to be prepared and focused, including yourself.

Downsize meetings to discussions

As a leader, I would prefer to have more discussions and fewer meetings. For me, they are different beasts, and so much time could be saved if we downsized some of our meetings to discussions. If we created some space in our schedule as a result, we could be more responsive to our team when they need our input.

I see a meeting as a formal tool designed to bring multiple people together to achieve an outcome. A discussion is less formal, is either 1:1 or involves just a few, and should be conducted in a much shorter timeframe, let's say ten minutes or less (see figure 7.3, overleaf). If you use this language with your team, and you are clear about the difference, responsiveness and availability improves across the team.

I also believe that discussions are best conducted in an alternative format to a meeting. For instance, meetings are usually held sitting down in a meeting room. If you do this with a discussion, you risk it feeling like (or actually turning into) a meeting. So, if it is a face-to-face discussion, have it standing up. It reminds

	Meeting	Discussion
Style	Formal	Informal
Location	Meeting Room	Standing or Phone
People	Many	1:1 or few
Duration	30 mins +	< 10 mins
Agenda	Multi-topic	Single topic
Result	Busy	Available

Figure 7.3: Meetings vs discussions

everyone involved that this is a short sharp discussion. If not face-to-face, then make it a phone call rather than an MS Teams video call. And if you say ten minutes, hold them to that. Don't let ten minutes become 30 minutes! Expect people to be organised for a short but focused discussion.

Make sure interruptions are productive ones

On the topic of availability, if you are interrupted with something urgent, make sure it is a productive interruption. Not like the time I interrupted Sir Bob Geldof!

The moment I met Bob Geldof was not as cool as it should have been — and it was my own fault. It was 1993, and I was backpacking my way around Australia. I ended up in Mildura picking grapes, and to my surprise, heard that Bob Geldof was coming to town.

He had been through a few years of Band Aid and Live Aid advocacy work and was wanting to get back to his music. Rather than book a capital city tour of Australia, he decided to tour the rural small towns with his new band.

So, being a fellow Dubliner, I bought tickets and went along with my mates. We were in the bar after the gig, and who do we see, but Sir Bob lining up for a drink. We cautiously approached and said, 'Hi Bob, we are from Dublin too, can we ask you a question?' He graciously replied, 'Hi lads, no problem. What do you want to ask me?'

Bloody hell, I had not expected that he would actually talk to us! I think the silicon chip inside my head got switched to overload! (If you are over 50, you will get what I did there.) I desperately tried to think of something profound to ask. Or at least intelligible. Remembering a story he told on stage about picking peas in a town like Mildura when he was younger, I blurted out, 'So Bob, did you really pick peas? Frozen peas or canned peas?'

I died inside as I saw his eyes glaze over. He was used to dealing with presidents, queens and rock stars, who I assume did not ask him about peas! He promptly excused himself (with a choice expletive, as I recall) and our moment passed.

In the workplace, I wonder how often we disappoint others with unprepared interruptions and half-baked thoughts and questions. And how often do we let others interrupt us in the same half-baked way?

Coach your team to interrupt you, and others, with the following in mind:

- If they ask for a minute, they should take a minute, not 20.

- Suggest they read the body language, and be mindful if it feels like it's not the best time to interrupt someone.

- Make sure they know the question they need to ask. They should be clear about what they are asking and be succinct in asking it.

- Get them to provide context, but not too much. Don't overwhelm people with background or their life story.

- Don't make others do the work. If it is an issue that they need solved, they should provide some recommended solutions rather than asking you or others to give them the answer.

Consider how your productivity style works with your teams'

One final thing to consider when working with your core team is how your productivity style works with their productivity style. Being aware of your own productivity biases can be really helpful when it comes to delegating work, having 1:1 discussions or collaborating with the team on joint work. Being aware of their biases can take your interactions to the next level.

If you identify as an Energiser, how does that play out when you delegate work? Or when you take on a new project with the team? Or when it comes to being available to them when they need you? If you are an Organiser, and they have a bias towards focus, how does that change the dynamic.

I once worked with a senior partner of a law firm who was definitely an Analyser. He was extremely intelligent, and one of the firm's best legal minds, but not great with people or at leading a team. He wanted to spend his time deeply focusing on legal problems, and got frustrated when he had to give direction to the team or manage or coach them in any way. His anxiety around this resulted in him micro-managing them too much, making life stressful for everyone involved.

I don't necessarily have the answers for you around how best to make your style work with your team's. But I do want to plant some of these questions in your mind, and get you to think about the interplays so you can come up with your own solutions for each of your team members.

Remember, do no harm

I opened part II with a reference to the Hippocratic Oath: First, do no harm. This requires you to do all of the things we have been talking about. Be responsive, be proactive, balance your schedule, create space to be available, set clear deadlines and expectations, delegate early. Be aware of the pitfalls of your productivity biases, especially if you are an Energiser who likes to leave things until the last minute. Use a system to manage your priorities proactively rather than reactively. Be aware of the disruption that your reactivity can have on your team.

And be careful about the stories you might tell yourself about working reactively, and the fact that you do your best work under pressure. I read a great Lanterna Education blog recently, 'The lie of working better under pressure', where the author of the blog suggests that students often procrastinate when working on assignments and studying for exams, and they tell themselves that they do their best work under pressure. They have clear memories of leaving work until the last minute, and then nailing the assignment or test anyway. But research suggests that, for many, this is just *memory bias* at work, where we only recall the positive outcomes, while conveniently forgetting the other times that we performed badly.

We may have gotten away with that sort of behaviour when we were at school or university, because it only affected us and our results. But if this is your workstyle when working in a team environment, your lack of planning will become an urgent distraction for your colleagues. Requesting information or delegating work at the last minute is one of the most selfish things you can do to your team or peers if the urgency could have been avoided by working more proactively.

● ● ●

Part II focused on two important partnerships. The first one is the one you make with your EA or executive support. Remember, you are two sides of the same coin when it comes to keeping you above the line, so invest some time in this partnership. Then focus on the second partnership between you and your direct reports or leadership team. Help them to be more productive, and help them to help you to be more productive.

In part III, we will look to the third productivity partnership, the one between you and your wider team. You have the opportunity to create and lead a more productive culture that benefits everyone and makes high levels of productivity more sustainable.

Reflections and intentions

- Are you as responsive and available as you should be?

- Are you struggling to be responsive because of email noise? If yes, what steps will you take to deal with this problem?

- Can your team get access to you easily if needed? Does this cause massive disruptions to your existing plans, or can you accommodate them easily?

- Think about your preferred productivity style (Organiser, Energiser, Analyser). How does your style impact how responsive or reactive you are?

PART III
YOUR TEAM

Enhanced productivity radiates outwards from you as a leader, through your direct reports and on to their wider teams. If you put the right strategies in place, you and your direct reports can greatly impact the productivity of your whole team. I have no doubt that your wider team will be extremely busy and will be feeling the pressure, just like you. This busyness may feel to them like they have too much work to do, and not enough capacity to get it all done.

I recently overheard a conversation between a team leader and the HR person who supported the team. They were discussing a pulse survey conducted across the team in question. One of the comments from the HR person caught my attention: *'A common theme coming through from all the respondents was that there is too much work for them to do. They feel overloaded all the time. We need to take this seriously and address this issue.'*

'Too much work' and *'not enough resources'* are phrases I hear a lot from workshop participants and clients. And sometimes, teams *are* asked to do too much, with too few resources to manage all the work. But to jump straight to the conclusion that there is too much work is a mistake in my view. In fact, before we ask, 'Is there too much work?' I believe we should ask two other, more useful questions related to what I call *capacity erosion*. Is there too much:

- *internal erosion* of our team's capacity?
- *external erosion* of our team's capacity?

Capacity erosion refers to the idea that we often allow our capacity to do productive work to be eroded away, bit by bit. Sometimes we do this to ourselves, and sometimes we allow others to do it to us. The *Cambridge Dictionary* defines capacity as, 'The total amount that can be contained or produced'. In this case, we are talking about the total amount of work that can be produced by an individual or a team. And I would further suggest we are talking about the total amount of work that can be produced in a reasonable number of hours. We can always get more done if we work longer, but that is not a sustainable solution to this problem.

Our capacity to do work is not just governed by time. As we have already discussed, our ability to get work done, and done well, requires not just time, but energy and focus. Of course, we need enough time to get things done, but if we have time, but don't have enough energy to do the task, it is really easy to switch off or procrastinate. If we don't have enough focus to apply to our work, we can easily allow ourselves to become distracted by other things.

But what if we had enough capacity to get all the required work done, but that capacity was being eroded by our own behaviours or the behaviours of others? What if our capacity was being attacked from within as well as from outside? The single most impactful thing a leader can do is to protect, and even enhance, the productive capacity of their team (see figure D, overleaf).

Internal capacity erosion

When we are not personally organised, we are at risk of eroding our own capacity. Think of your personal work capacity like a suitcase — a container that can only fit so many things. If there are too many things to fit easily, then we might feel we have no choice but to leave some things out. But if we take the time to fold and organise the contents well, we can fit more into the space. I know this to be true as my partner, Vera, is a ninja packer! Organising the contents well allows us to maximise the capacity of the suitcase.

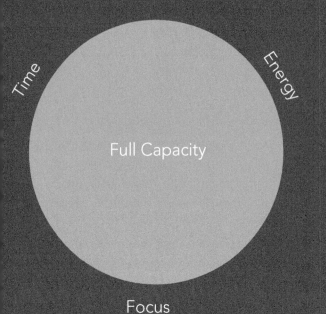

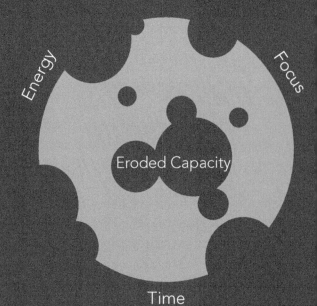

Figure D: Productivity erosion

Likewise, when we have a good organising system for our work, we have more capacity to get stuff done. Your team members protect their productive capacity when they are organised. But if they are not organised, they create a way of working that makes them feel busy and stressed, with a lot of wasted time, energy and focus. Some examples of things that internally erode capacity might be:

- not having an effective system for managing priorities

- being sloppy with calendar commitments and events

- reacting to emails and distracting alerts

- using the inbox as a messy filing system and task list

- working reactively and leaving work until the last minute.

All these examples erode your team's capacity to get important work done. The good news is these personal productivity issues are easily remedied with some basic training or coaching. It amazes me sometimes how, as workers, we are often expected to be highly productive with little formal guidance on how to do this. So, if this is an issue in your team, organise some training for them. It is such a good investment. But I am hoping that this section will also provide you with lots of strategies to coach them to protect their capacity.

External capacity erosion

Of course, many people are highly organised, but experience a different form of capacity erosion—one created by the people around them, and by the culture they work within. Every time we receive an email, phone call, Microsoft Teams message, meeting invite, interruption or delegation, we are at risk of capacity erosion. When other people are not mindful and purposeful in their interactions with us, it can cause our productivity to drop, and can divert our time, energy and focus to less important things. Unproductive cultures allow friction to thrive, which always erodes capacity. Some examples of this might be:

- last-minute urgent meeting invites that disrupt our plans

- too much email noise due to poor use of email

- thoughtless and unnecessary interruptions

- poorly designed work processes

- other people creating urgency by leaving critical work until the last minute.

Working with others is complex, and it would be impossible to completely solve this problem. But this type of capacity erosion can be greatly reduced with a bit of effort. Unfortunately, many teams have not stopped to examine the different ways that capacity is being eroded across their team. Investing time in raising awareness about the behaviours that cause erosion and putting team agreements in place to shift behaviours is well worthwhile, in my opinion. When we influence group behaviours in a positive way, we create more productive cultures. Read on…

CHAPTER 8
Lead productive cultures

When I wrote *Smart Teams* in 2018, I concluded that productivity was more than just a set of personal skills and strategies. For sustained productivity to truly exist for a team, the individuals in the team need to work in cultures that don't just support productivity, but allow it to flourish. I identified three distinct productivity cultures, which are the team's:

- communication culture

- meeting culture

- collaboration culture.

My premise was that when these cultures are healthy, productivity flourishes, and when they are unhealthy, they languish.

As is the way when writing books, soon after publication I realised that my theory was incomplete. There is a fourth culture that is crucial to team productivity: the team's urgency culture. Many organisations I work with have highly reactive cultures, and this also kills productivity. This led to me write *Urgent!* in 2020 to complete my thinking on productivity cultures. Except, of course, my thinking was not complete, as another ingredient is required to create sustainable productivity cultures: leaders who buy into the approach and lead productive cultures. So, here we are.

As I said previously, I cannot think of a more impactful thing that a leader can do than to increase the capacity of their team, and allow them to excel in their roles in a way that supports their balance and wellbeing. Beyond how you interface with your team, this involves helping them to work with each other, and with all of the other parts of your organisation in a productive way. As we will see in chapter 9, it also involves opening the space to be accountable and to hold others to account on a set of working agreements, which are the key to creating productive cultures. It involves giving them the tools to battle busyness, urgency, disorganisation and distraction.

By working on your *communication* culture, you can reduce the noise created through the overuse and poor use of email, MS Teams messages and other communication platforms.

By working on your *meeting* culture, you can reduce the number of unnecessary meetings and improve the quality of the meetings that are necessary.

By working on your *collaboration* culture, you can make work more visible across the team and reduce the friction that comes from collaborating on complex work.

By working on your *urgency* culture, you can reduce unnecessary urgency and create an importance mindset that serves your team better. All of these cultures require leadership, and may require a less self-centred approach from you and your team.

Self-centred or others-centred?

A good starting point to get on the path of leading more productive cultures is to consider some research that was conducted by Ryan Byerly, Peter Hill and Keith Edwards of the University of Sheffield in the UK in 2021. Their research led them to the conclusion that teams that had a high number of *others-centred* members versus *self-centred* members were more productive and collaborated more effectively.

They describe others-centredness as the tendency to put other people's interests ahead of their own when they can't equally promote their own interests and the other party's. They value their own interests highly, but also value interpersonal relationships and are willing to serve the other person's interests in specific circumstances to foster the relationship.

The research test they conducted involved placing people in pairs, giving one of the pairs five $2 bills. They then asked that person to divide the money as evenly as possible between the pair, without cutting any of the bills in half. So, they were faced with a choice. Do they keep three of the $2 bills for themselves, and give the other person two bills, or do they keep two of the bills for themselves and give away the other three bills?

The ones who decided to keep the higher amount for themselves were labelled as 'self-centred', as they chose to serve their interests over the other person's. Those who only kept two of the bills were labelled 'others-centred', as they served the other person's interests over their own. In this experiment, it is important to note that the others-centred people were not totally selfless, giving all of the money to the other party. And I suspect, if they could have achieved a 50:50 split, they might have chosen that option.

I reckon that this has huge implications for how we create and lead productive cultures. If we can coach our teams to operate with an others-centred mindset, they are more likely to work in a way that is productive for themselves as well as for those around them.

I explored a similar concept in *Smart Teams*, where I cited the Nash equilibrium as one of the keys to reducing productivity friction within our team. Made famous in the movie *A Beautiful Mind*, John Nash's contribution to the field of game theory thinking was that the best result comes from everyone doing what is best for themselves and for the group at the same time. This is often termed as 'win/win', and it has many applications, including in how we work and collaborate.

If we approach our work in a self-centred way, or in a win/lose way, we create productivity friction. Every time we send an email, there is a risk that we will create productivity friction for the recipients, especially if we copy them in unnecessarily, or don't take the time to write the email in an easily digestible way. Every time we call a meeting, there is a risk of productivity friction if we don't invite the right people, don't take the time to focus the meeting with a clear purpose, or don't run the meeting to time. This friction is created a thousand times a day across our team, and it feels like a death by a thousand cuts. And, of course, this friction causes capacity erosion.

But if we cultivate a culture where our team strives to adopt an others-centred mindset, we firmly place value on the interpersonal relationships within the team, and on the productivity of the team as a whole. This reduces the productivity friction across the team, allowing everyone to operate at a higher level of effectiveness. How good is that?

Team agreements are the link between intentions and behaviours

One of the challenges often faced by teams that want to create more productive cultures is that they may have the best intentions, but they don't live up to them. Their behaviours do not match their intentions. This gap between intention and behaviour is widened when the team gets busy, stressed or overwhelmed. This is where *team agreements* come in. When you agree as a team how you intend to work together, it provides a mechanism to hold yourselves and others to account on a way of working and collaborating.

Much of the work my team and I do with clients is around team cultures and team agreements. Once we have helped each member of a team to become personally productive, we then shift the focus to their productivity cultures. We don't try to shift all four cultures at once, but rather tackle them one at a time, which will be my advice to you. We aim to help them create a bespoke set of team agreements for, as an example, their communication culture, with the aim of reducing email noise across the team, and we put a three-month project in place to shift the culture. A one-page team agreements document is the key to accountability in your team workplace, be it physical or remote. These agreements are simple and practical, but can be powerful if developed in the right way.

The role of agreements

Team agreements, if created deliberately to counter the productivity pains being experienced by the team, serve to create a strong link between our good intentions and our actual behaviours. We can have the best intentions in the world, but sometimes there is a gap between these intentions and what we actually do on a day-to-day basis. Before we get to that gap, let's take a step back. Let's start with a shared purpose.

*Team agreements
are the link between
good intentions and
actual behaviours.*

Gathering your team to discuss the productivity friction they may be experiencing, and creating a shared purpose, is a great starting point for creating a healthier team culture. My friend Alex Hagen, whom I mentioned in chapter 1 in relation to a bias for focus, is a futurist who works with organisations to help them thrive in a fast-changing world. He reckons one of the biggest challenges many organisations face is creating a tangible link between the vision of the organisation, and what people are working on day-to-day. When there is a shared purpose and everyone in the team is aligned, people work better together and great things are achieved.

Similarly, when it comes to shifting productivity cultures, we need to start with a shared purpose, a clear vision of the problems we are solving and the benefit to the team in doing this work. A shared purpose in this context is created by, firstly, talking to the team about what productivity issues they believe they are facing. If you were to work on your meeting culture, it would be a good idea to understand exactly how your team is feeling about the quantity and quality of the meetings they experience in their role.

Once you can define the key issues that need to be addressed, your team will begin to buy into a shared purpose. I believe that a shared problem can only be solved by a shared effort, and I am sure that most of your team will be feeling similar pain when it comes to productivity. Some useful questions to ask your team to create a shared purpose are:

- What causes you productivity pain when it comes to (insert communications, meetings, collaboration, urgency)?

- What are the consequences of this productivity friction for our team?

- If we were to shift this culture for the team, what would that look like?

Once you are clear about the issues to be addressed, it's a good idea to identify what success would look like if you were to create a more productive culture. Understanding what success would look like is critical to successful change initiatives. My fitness trainer, Adrienne, often gets me to do mini exercises to isolate muscles so that I can feel what it is like when that muscle is engaged. She then tells me that I need to be aware of that feeling when I am doing a workout, because when that muscle is engaged, I am doing the exercise correctly and getting the most benefit from it. Same in your organisation. Knowing what good behaviours look and feel like helps your team to know when they are on or off track.

The project that you will put in place to shift your culture will take effort and discipline from all of your team. They will only bother to do the work if they can buy into the *why* and can hold that shared vision in their minds.

Our shared purpose should drive our good intentions (see figure 8.1). Ideally, we would embrace the ideal of *others-centredness* once we have bought into the vision for the greater good of the team and, of course, ourselves.

Our actual behaviours are what drive culture. In fact, someone once said to me that culture is just a set of group behaviours. What we see people doing and saying on a day-to-day basis is what shapes our culture. When I see attendees from an organisation consistently turning up late to training sessions, that tells me something about their culture. When I get unnecessarily copied into emails from a client to my business manager that tells me something about the culture of that team.

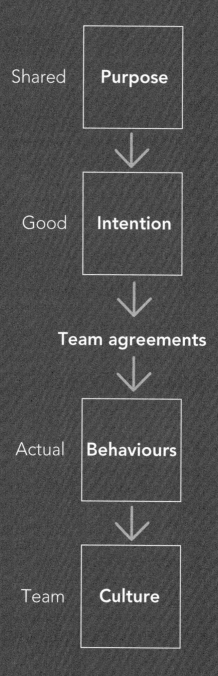

Figure 8.1: Team agreements chain

So, our shared purpose drives our good intentions. Our actual behaviour drives our team culture. But what bridges the gap? How can we make sure our good intentions drive our actual behaviours?

When we get busy, stressed or overwhelmed, our behaviours might not match our intentions. At these times the system may break down as we revert to less-than-ideal, possibly self-centred behaviours.

Now I am sure very few people come to work intending to cause productivity friction for their team and colleagues. We don't set out to be late to meetings, or to create unnecessary email noise, or to leave things until the last minute. We have the best of intentions, but we are only human. This is where team agreements come in. They bridge the gap between good intentions and actual behaviours, because they make us all more accountable.

Team agreements may create a critical link in the chain, but we need to do the work as a team to create them in the first place, and then they need to be led from the top to keep them alive. I have seen so many change initiatives around productivity culture that last only a few months, or even a few weeks, because the leaders in the team were absent from the process, or even worse, ignored the team agreements as if they were above having to adhere to this way of working. This is cultural change, and this type of initiative needs strong and committed leadership.

When we get this right, our shared purpose sets the team's good intentions. Our good intentions are embodied in the team agreements. The team agreements drive our actual behaviours, and our behaviours set the productivity culture.

What form should team agreements take?

There are many names for team agreements in different workplaces. Some call them rules, some call them protocols, some call them a charter. I like the word 'agreement' as it signifies that these have been created by the team, for the team. We have all agreed to a way of working and a set of standards.

To that end, I believe that team agreements should be worded as an agreed behaviour. 'We will focus meetings with an agenda' is much more compelling than 'Meeting agendas to be used for meetings'. The slight bit of context in the statement also helps people to remember that we are trying to *focus* the meeting. Sometimes adding a qualifying statement with the agreement, or some examples of how we will execute the agreed behaviour, can be also helpful.

Example 1: We will focus meetings with an agenda.

- Use a meeting agenda to plan and run the meeting in a focused and productive way. This should be shared with participants in a timely way.

Example 2: We will set clear meeting objectives.

- Outline the purpose and objective of the meeting when sending the invitation.

- Start every meeting by restating and agreeing on the meeting objective.

- For each meeting objective, ask what, who and why. Understand what you're solving, *who* is the accountable decision-maker and why we need to achieve this objective.

How many agreements are enough? Having too many agreements can make it difficult for people to remember them easily, and therefore, follow them. A rule of thumb for me is five to six agreed behaviours that will fit on one A4 page. These should be the most impactful agreements that your team agree on to solve the productivity pain points you have identified.

It is always a good idea to get someone in the team or your marketing department to design the agreements as a small poster, a screensaver or even a mouse mat (do we still use those?). Make it visible for everyone, but most importantly, keep talking about it. Get everyone to buy into it and find a way to enshrine it within the fabric of the team.

Some teams like to create a poster and have everyone in the team sign it to show commitment to this way of working. Some teams make this a topic at their weekly team meeting, to check in on how people are going in sticking to the agreements, and talk about what benefits they are experiencing as a result. Share some good news stories, or even have a prize for best behaviours of the week.

It is a part of your role as a leader to keep the fire burning for this project. If you see the flames dimming, stoke the fire and put some more wood on. But you don't need to do this alone. Many teams identify three to four internal champions who not only keep the agreements in people's minds, but can also serve as coaches for those who may need a bit of help to shift their behaviours.

If you do make it a three-month project, it is probably worth having a review after the three months to see what has changed. If you identified a measure of success, have you achieved it? If not, what got in the way? Is this plate spinning now, freeing you up to look at another culture, and get another plate spinning? Or do you need to give the plate an additional spin?

Here are a few examples of team agreements for your communication, meeting, collaboration and urgency cultures to get you and your team started.

Communication agreements

- Make it easy for the reader.

- Ensure the subject line makes sense.

- Use Cc and Reply All with purpose.

- Be responsive, not reactive to email.

- Agree on the most appropriate tools for communication.

Meeting agreements

- Only use meetings when they are required.

- Focus the meeting with an agenda.

- Run 'on time' meetings.

- Invite participants not spectators.

- Always state the meeting purpose.

Collaboration agreements

- Seek alignment when collaborating.

- Reduce unnecessary interruptions and distractions.

- Manage project work proactively.

- Agree on the best collaboration tools for your team.

- Own your part of the outcome.

Urgency agreements

- Consider importance before urgency.

- Avoid creating unnecessary urgency for others.

- Use appropriate tools for urgent requests.

- Do what you say you are going to do.

- Be mindful of other people's workloads.

Your role as a leader in shifting the culture

As the leader, you have a responsibility to explicitly lead productivity within the team. The behaviours you model, the expectations you set and the conversations you have around your productivity cultures will make or break the required changes. A people leader has five key roles in leading the cultural change, and these are to:

- *inspire* the team with a compelling vision

- clearly *communicate* the expectations around team agreements

- consistently *call out* unacceptable behaviours

- personally *model* the behaviours agreed on by the team

- *keep* the cultural change firmly on the agenda over time.

I am a huge advocate for team agreements, and the way they can create a cultural shift for your team. You may not change the culture of your whole organisation, but you can create a micro-culture within your team that has a positive impact, and creates ripples that influence the teams around you. But one of the keys to sustaining team agreements over time is also having a culture of empowerment and accountability within the team. That is where we are going to go in the next chapter.

Reflections and intentions

- Do you feel your team operates more often in an others-centred way or a self-centred way?

- Which would be your team's most challenging productivity culture?

- When will you have a conversation with your direct reports about your team's productivity cultures?

- Think about your preferred productivity style (Organiser, Energiser, Analyser). How does your style impact the culture of your team?

CHAPTER 9

Create a contract of trust

Trust is a keystone for any productive relationship between a leader and their team, and between each of the team members. It's a bit of a platitude, and I know you have heard this a thousand times, but without trust, productivity suffers as we seek to blame others and to protect our interests at all costs. Without trust, others-centredness cannot exist. And without trust, team agreements will not have any impact in the long run.

Two ingredients need to be in place for team trust to exist: Reliability and accountability. One is the responsibility of the leader, and the other the responsibility of the team. The team needs reliability from their leader, and needs to be able to trust that their leader will be clear and predictable. In turn, the leader needs their team to be accountable, and to take ownership of their work and results.

Two ingredients need to be in place for trust to exist: Reliability and accountability. One is the responsibility of the leader, and the other the responsibility of the team.

My partner, Vera, is a senior finance executive and has managed teams across the world. When I shared my thinking on this with her, she said, 'I call this my contract with my team.' I pushed her to explain, and she told me that one of the tools she uses with every team member is to sit down with them and discuss the contract they need to create to work effectively together. It basically says that you can rely on me and I can rely on you if we work this way. Now, of course, she does not get them to sign a contract, it is a verbal agreement, a shared understanding about expectations, and is different to team agreements. This is a shared understanding, set up from the start. This is what I call a *contract of trust* (see figure 9.1, overleaf).

Trust, driven by accountability and reliability, is the grease that oils the wheels of effective team collaboration. Let's start by looking how you can create a culture of accountability within your team (which, of course, includes yourself, as you also need to be accountable), and then at the things you need to commit to if you want to be reliable.

Accountable culture

If we look at accountability on a spectrum, we might find that it takes its place as the healthy centre of two less-than-ideal possible cultures: Freedom and control. All three possible cultures will be most likely driven by the leader (see figure 9.2, on page 190).

In a *freedom* culture, members of the team are given too much power to decide how they work. This may be fine most of the time if you have an experienced and well-calibrated team, but if they're not experienced, or if they're overwhelmed by workload and pressure, the risk is they adopt a *selfish* mindset, working

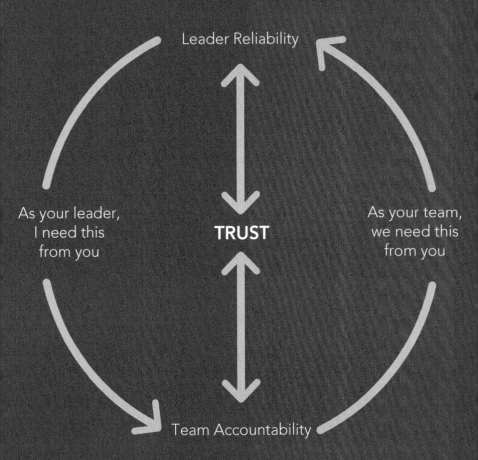

Leader Reliability

TRUST

As your leader,
I need this
from you

As your team,
we need this
from you

Team Accountability

Figure 9.1: The contract of trust

the way they want to work, with little regard for others' needs. This is similar to the concept of self-centred versus others-centred ways of working.

If this is the prevailing operating mindset, then the team works very independently of each other, looking after their own patch. One of the things that may have led to this situation is a disengaged leader who just lets people do their own thing. You will probably find that the driving force in this scenario is looking after number one, which will never create a good foundation for trust. If everyone can just do what they want, it can become a bit like the Wild West, with no rules, or rules that are ignored because they are not enforced.

At the other end of the spectrum you have a *control* culture. In this case, the personal mindset of the team members is *selfless*; they do whatever they are told, even if it frustrates them or forces them to compromise. How many workers compromise their work/life balance because they feel they have no agency or power to change it? Again, the leader is likely to be driving the culture.

In this scenario, the team dynamic could be fearful, as their leader, or leadership in general, maintains strict control and enforces it. The leadership style is likely to be micro-managing, and the driving force, authority: 'I will tell you what to do, how to do it and when to do it.' Again, not ideal if you want to build a culture of trust, and certainly not ideal if you want to maximise the outputs of your highly talented team.

It was so interesting to see these dynamics play out over the last few years as we went through COVID, and the ensuing work-from-home restrictions. Many organisations struggled with how they maintained control of their people and their work when they could no longer see them at their desks.

	Freedom Culture	Accountable Culture	Control Culture
Driving Force	SELF INTEREST I am busy looking after me	INFLUENCE I inspire you to do great work	AUTHORITY I tell you what you need to do
Leadership Style	DISENGAGED I assume you are doing the work	EMPOWERING I enable you to do your work	MICRO-MANAGING I make sure you do the work
Team Dynamic	INDEPENDENT We look out for ourselves	SUPPORTIVE We look out for each other	FEARFUL We look over our shoulders
Personal Mindset	SELFISH I do what I want to do	SERVING I do what needs to be done	SELFLESS I do what I am told to do

Figure 9.2: Accountable culture framework

Many organisations saw an increase in the number of meetings, and the volume of email as a result, as a way of maintaining some level of perceived control. Some even introduced monitoring software so they could tell how many hours workers were at their desk or using their laptop.

Many organisations eventually realised that their people were being just as productive, if not more productive, working from home, and eased up on the control mechanisms. But it left a residue, and we are still battling to reduce the number of meetings and the volume of emails, as these volumes became the new normal.

I suspect the teams that fared the best in this period were teams that already had an accountable culture in place, or were able to build one quickly when faced with the COVID challenge. In an accountable culture, the individuals have a *serving* mindset, doing what needs to be done, but serving their needs and the team's needs as best they can. They are supportive and look out for each other, adopting an other-mindedness approach. The leadership style is empowering, as the leader strives to enable the team to do their own work, and make their own decisions where appropriate.

Finally, the driving force behind how an accountable team operates is influence. Not positional power or rules and regulations, but the true power that comes through inspiration, respect and trust. I want to work in a team like that!

Accountability and team agreements

When you create team agreements, and you set out to create a cultural change within your team that will be sustained over time, it is crucial that your team is both accountable and empowered. The team agreements serve as something we can all hold ourselves to account on, as well as hold other people to account on.

When it comes to holding each other to account, an empowered team, a truly empowered team, will be comfortable calling out poor behaviours in a respectful way, whoever is the perpetrator. As a leader, you should also be accountable to the agreements, and should be OK if your team call you out when you don't comply. Your team also needs to be able to call each other out without involving you, and without causing a conflict. Having an open discussion with your team about this can be useful. Making it OK for everyone in the team to be able to call out poor behaviours is a very powerful empowerment strategy.

This is something that we have come to see more and more in high-performance cultures like sporting teams. I am sure this is not new for them, but our access to what is said behind the closed doors of top sporting teams has become greater and greater through some of the documentaries that have aired over the past few years. We have been allowed into the hallowed changing rooms of football teams, cricket teams, Formula 1 racing teams and AFL footy teams. Sometimes you will see them debrief a poor game or race in these programs, providing the players a safe space and process to call teammates out on poor behaviours or lack of effort. They do it respectfully, and always with a view to improving how they operate as a team. It's not just the coach's role to call out poor behaviours, but the whole team's. And, of course, often it is the player themselves putting their hand up to say, 'Sorry, I should have done better.'

The trust required for team agreements to work in a sustainable way can be summed up for both the leaders and the team.

The leader needs their team to:

- be accountable
- deliver on commitments and deadlines
- put their hand up if they are struggling
- ask questions if they need clarification
- manage up and negotiate
- learn from mistakes
- escalate appropriately
- do their part of the work
- learn to fight their own battles
- make the leader's life easier if they can.

As a leader, when I can trust that this is how my team will operate, I feel confident in empowering them to manage their work and make reasonable decisions without too much input from me. In turn, I understand that they need reliability from me.

The team needs their leader to:

- be reliable
- say what they mean, mean what they say
- back them up if needed
- not undermine them
- set and manage expectations
- communicate clearly

- set reasonable priorities and deadlines

- act with integrity

- empower them

- not micro-manage them.

When your team can trust that this is how you will operate, they can step up and be accountable with confidence.

Fix the problem or fix the process

Unfortunately, sometimes the problem cannot be fixed by simply getting the team to be accountable. Sometimes we need to fix the process. If a problem keeps recurring, you may need to look beyond your people and fix the process or system.

I read about a train crash in the UK that should have been avoided with the use of a simple indicator ring placed in the track switch lever. If a train was stopped on the secondary track near the station, the indicator ring would remind everyone that a train was parked on the side track. It was there for good reason, but no one ever used it and there had never been a problem in the past. Until, one day, there was a problem, which led to a catastrophic crash.

The resultant investigation led to the realisation that there is often a gap between work imagined and work done. The people who wrote the rulebook imagined that the safety indicator ring would be used, consistently, every time. But the work done, the reality, was different. People got lazy over time. In the world of safety, they now put a lot of focus on closing the gap between the work imagined and the work done.

We can use this lesson to fix problems that may come from us simply being human. Humans will always make mistakes, get stressed, cut corners, get overwhelmed and forget things. So rather than blame the people, it might be worth changing the process to account for human behaviours and human shortcomings. My mantra is that if it happens once, fix the problem; if it keeps happening, fix the process. But this requires everyone in the team be accountable to look out for instances of this, and empowered to raise it with the right people to create the necessary change.

● ● ●

Productive and effective work practices rely on accountability and empowerment—and trust. So it's a good idea to create a contract of trust with each of your team members. Make this one of the first things you do when a new member joins the team. Make it something that you discuss in your performance evaluation meetings. Praise people when you see them doing something good in this respect. And consistently call out less-than-ideal behaviours.

Reflections and intentions

- Do you trust your team to deliver what you need?
- Have you fostered a culture of accountability?
- Are you a reliable leader?
- Do you have a contract of trust in place with your team?
- Think about your preferred productivity style (Organiser, Energiser, Analyser). How does your style impact the trust between you and your team?

PART IV
External Interface

We have explored how productivity radiates out from you as a leader, through your direct reports and on to your wider team. But, of course, it does not stop there. Just as there is an interface between you and your team that can be productive or disruptive, there is an interface between you and the rest of your organisation, and an interface between your team and the rest of the organisation that can also impact productivity.

If we took a siloed approach to productivity improvement, we would only focus on ourselves and our team, which would bring limited results. This is because we are interacting with other stakeholders every day who communicate with us, meet with us, and collaborate with us. We work interdependently with so many different individuals and groups that it just makes sense to think about how we can also reduce friction when working with them.

The challenge here is that you don't have any control over these other teams. In *Smart Teams* I talked about the idea that the only thing you can control is your own personal productivity. You have some level of control with your team, and you can and should lead your team's productivity. But, you have no control over those inside your organisation but outside of your team, your peers and their teams. You need to *influence* them, to inspire them to work on their productivity culture, and in some cases, have respectful negotiations with them where clear expectations are agreed and boundaries are set.

In this final section, we will look at the interface between you and your team, and the rest of the organisation, and the opportunity you have to truly inspire a major uplift in productivity across the wider organisation.

CHAPTER 10

Practice respectful negotiation

Everything in this life is a negotiation. We negotiate with ourselves, with our family, with the dog, with our team, with our peers, with other teams, with our stakeholders, and with our clients. And that is as it should be. Negotiation is not a battle, and should not be a negative thing. Respectful negotiation is how we get things done in a way that equally serves us and the other stakeholders involved. Respectful negotiation speaks of equality, of finding a win/win. I like to think of this type of negotiation as collaborative negotiation rather than adversarial negotiation.

On a recent trip to Europe, I experienced collaborative negotiation in action while having lunch with friends in Amsterdam. We spent a weekend with our friends Tiziana and Eric, who showcased their beautiful city so well, especially when they took us on the canals in their boat. On the Sunday, they organised a surprise lunch, which involved taking the boat through the city canals, out to the Amstel river and to a small village on the outskirts of the city.

We pulled up to a dock outside the restaurant, and made our way in for an Indonesian feast (which it turns out, is pretty much the Dutch national cuisine, as Indonesia was a Dutch colony). On arrival, Tiziana and Eric looked a bit disappointed, as the table they had sat at last time by the water was occupied. The one we were allocated was not just away from the waterfront, but it was in the full sun. When they booked, they had asked for a waterfront table, which are all under cover. So, Eric masterfully went into what I would call a collaborative negotiation.

He did not get irate or make demands, but rather invited the manager to work with him to find a solution. He said that he was fine not being by the water, but would prefer not to sit in the sun. He asked, '*What could we do to make that possible?*' After some discussion, the manager talked to his team, and then suggested that they could move our table into another space that was not in the sun. A few minutes later we were sitting in a very acceptable position having an exceptional lunch.

I reckon the key to Eric's successful negotiation was the collaborative nature of it. There was no 'I want', or 'You should', but rather 'How could' and 'What if'. I love the question he asked. It was not an ultimatum, but an invitation to think outside the box. It was not closed and threatening, but open and explorative. Eric invited the manager to work with him to solve the problem in a way that worked for his restaurant team and for us.

Negotiating with other teams

You, and of course your team, will need to negotiate with other parts of the organisation on a daily basis. One challenge that I often hear in relation to this is that other teams want work to be delivered as *good* as possible, as *soon* as possible. They don't always consider your team's other priorities, existing deadlines or the fact that this possibly urgent request is unreasonable because it was left until the last minute. Positional power often then comes into play, and more senior managers put pressure on your more junior team members to get what they want. Or sometimes, your team members assume urgency just because it is coming from someone 'important'. Or someone just screams loud enough to get what they want. The squeaky wheel gets the oil.

These examples are negotiations as well, but they are adversarial negotiations, where someone needs to compromise to please the other. With practice, there is a better way to turn a potentially adversarial negotiation into a collaborative one.

When I wrote the book *Urgent!*, I wanted to give people a way of recognising and dealing with unreasonable urgency. Urgency is one of the things we have to negotiate more than anything else in the workplace, and many people end up working extremely reactively trying to deal with all of the urgent requests that come their way each day. Urgency is unavoidable, but if you really examine what is happening with urgency, much of it is either fake or avoidable.

I suggest using a tool that I call the Urgency Dials, where you try to find out what is negotiable for the other party if the deadline is not. Or, if nothing else is negotiable, help them to see that some flexibility on the deadline might be the only option. Imagine a set of knobs or levers that you can turn up or down, like the music equaliser on your old stereo unit. These knobs allow you to work out what can be adjusted to aid with the negotiation. Some negotiation knobs might be:

- time or the deadline itself

- quality of the output

- scope of the work

- available resources to do the work

- budget and financial resources or constraints

- risk appetite of the stakeholder.

For example, if another team needed some analysis urgently from your team by Friday, you might negotiate on the scope or quality of the analysis. You could suggest that they could have a basic analysis by Friday or a more in-depth analysis in a week. Note: I am not saying have your team do poor-quality work, just that quality is a negotiable.

Like the marshmallow choice mentioned in chapter 7, this gives the other party the choice, but makes it clear that they cannot expect to have the work to the highest level of quality at a moment's notice. My old sales manager used to say you can have it good, cheap or fast. Pick two!

In one of the episodes of *The Crown* on Netflix, the British Prime Minister John Major tells Prince Charles that there are two languages being spoken in a negotiation. The one on the surface, and the one underneath that describes what the person really wants. He says he prefers to ignore the first and just work on the latter.

Time is one of your negotiables, and quality is a second. You can have it fast or good. These are the most common factors that are used in workload negotiations. But complementing these two core negotiables are scope, resources, budget and even risk. They are all negotiable and will hold a value to you, and a value to your negotiating counterpart. A respectful negotiation will involve a conversation that explores what is negotiable and what is not, before agreeing a course of action that serves the work and both parties. It is worth going beyond the surface-level demand (this is urgent) to what the person really needs, which might be something different.

Other negotiables

Although I find urgency to be the most common negotiable that my clients discuss with me when we talk about productivity issues, it is not the only thing your team needs to negotiate. Some useful negotiation-focused questions might be:

- Is this work that we should be doing?

- What is the opportunity cost for us if we take this on?

- What is the win/win for us and them?

- Is there a part of the work that the other team should do, and part that we should do?

- Are there other resources that we could draw upon to get this done?

It is important to note that respectful negotiation is not about saying 'no' to everything. I sometimes think people shy away from strategies like this as they think it will make them seem like a difficult person to work with. Done badly, that might be the outcome. But done well, it is a strategy that makes people want to work with you. I would prefer people to negotiate with me and then deliver as promised, than not negotiate and not deliver anyway!

This is such a valuable skill to coach in your team. If you have done the work to empower your team to manage their own work and make their own decisions, then they are ripe to be able to negotiate their own workloads. And that means they are empowered to negotiate with you, with each other and with other teams.

One specific area of workload negotiation to coach your team on is meeting attendance. Have you ever thought about the minimum requirements that need to be met before a meeting invite should be accepted? To be more discerning about meetings, you and your team need to be really clear about whether a meeting meets the minimum criteria that would allow the red velvet rope to be unhooked to enable access to your busy schedules. Being available should not be the only requirement that needs to be met to make it into your schedule:

- The first question to ask yourselves is: *Is this a good use of my/our time?* If the meeting is not a good strategic fit, you need to push back.

- Consider the opportunity cost. Will this create a scheduling clash with something already in the calendar? Does it deserve to override the other meeting? Even if you or your team members are available, that day or that week may already be full, and this is tipping you beyond your 'do not fill above this level' line.

- Have the meeting organisers clearly communicated the purpose and objective of the meeting? If not, how can you be sure that this meeting will be a good use of your time? You may not decline the meeting invite, but in this case, I would at least push back for some more information before committing.

- Are you really the one needed in this meeting? Could or should it be another member of the team, or someone from another team altogether? Are you being invited for the right reasons, or just to serve someone else's agenda or preferences?

- Is a meeting even necessary, or could the topic be dealt with in some other way? Would an email, a Teams chat or a quick discussion be a better option than a more formal and time-consuming meeting?

One of the mindsets that can help you be more discerning when evaluating meeting invites is to look at the decision in a more holistic way than just available/unavailable. Being available doesn't mean you should give that time away. Discussing these strategies as a team is a great way to build a united front and an aligned way of negotiating meetings.

Whether your team members are negotiating with people in your own team or with other teams and stakeholders, avoid being dragged into too many negotiations on behalf of your team members. There are always situations where you will expect them to escalate the issue to you, and you should coach the team on using escalation as a tool, as you as a leader can increase the priority of a piece of work in the eyes of your peers. But your team needs to be careful to only escalate when necessary, not as a first port of call. They should be able to do their own negotiating for the most part.

There will be times where you will need to step in and negotiate on behalf of your team. In some ways, one of your roles is running defence (an American football term) for your team, and protecting them from the frictions created by the organisation so they can focus fully on what they do best.

Sometimes your role is to inspire them to hold the line in the face of busyness, urgency, disorganisation and distraction.

There is a great scene in the movie *Braveheart*, where William Wallace (Mel Gibson) steadies his men on the battlefield, as the better-equipped and larger English force bears down on them. As his rag-tag Scottish army stands in a long line waiting for the enemy, he calls 'Hold, hold, hold the line'. His men are nervous, but they do hold, inspired by his bravery and leadership. The oncoming English are overpowered by the brave Scots, who win the day in the face of a seemingly impossible onslaught.

As we face the daily onslaught of requests and deadlines, emails and meeting invitations, we need to find the conviction and courage to hold the line, and not give in to the pressure. Sometimes we need to hold the line and stay with what we believe to be the more important use of our time, rather than getting diverted from our priorities. Easier said than done, but with strong and inspiring leaders who lead by example, and coach their teams to fight for their priorities, it is possible. That's you, by the way!

William Wallace made a stand against the tyranny of the English and said enough is enough! He inspired his team to hold in the face of enormous pressure. *'They may take our lives, but they'll never take our freedom!'*

Think about how you, as a leader, could inspire your team to stay focused on your team's priorities. Trust, empowerment and accountability will help. Alignment of priorities and an understanding of the bigger picture will also help. These all take time to develop in your team, but isn't this what you should

As we face the daily onslaught of requests and deadlines, emails and meeting invitations, we need to find the conviction and courage to hold the line, and not give in to the pressure.

be doing as a leader? Isn't this more important than some of the meetings you find yourself in day in day out?

• • •

OK, almost there. We have explored the productivity of you. We have explored your role in creating productive partnerships with your direct reports, and we have explored how you can create more productive cultures for your wider team to work within.

You will hopefully end up with a super-productive team, working effectively and efficiently, and achieving great things. But do you want your team to be a productive bubble in a sea of less than productive teams? There is an opportunity here to inspire the teams around you to go next-level with their productivity too.

The final chapter will explore how you can inspire your peers and stakeholders, and the teams that surround you, to work with you and your team in a more productive way. I would like to inspire you to become a true champion for elite productivity within your organisation, who will in time inspire those around them.

Reflections and intentions

- Does your team suffer from too much urgency pressure from the business?

- What strategies could you share with your team to help them negotiate their workloads and deadlines more effectively?

- Do you inspire your team to hold the line?

- Think about your preferred productivity style (Organiser, Energiser, Analyser). How does your style enhance or hamper negotiations with others?

CHAPTER 11
Inspire your peers

Some leaders just shine. I get to work with a lot of people in my role, in many different organisations, many of whom are senior managers and leaders. I love my clients, and for the most part, get to work with smart, driven, passionate people who are open to learning and growing. But some leaders just stand above the rest for me — they demonstrate true leadership in everything they do.

One of those people is Chris Cowley, who was the regional GM of a global medical equipment manufacturer based in Dubai when I last worked with him. I had worked with Chris and his team in Australia a few years before, and when Chris moved into the regional role in Dubai, he asked me to fly over to work with his new leadership team there.

It was a great trip, and we did of mix of work on the leadership team's personal productivity, as well as some work creating team agreements for the communication and meeting cultures. Chris was a great support in the lead-up to the training, as although he was busy, he made it a priority to frame the vision for the training with his team, helped me design the agenda, and participated in the training himself, even though he had already experienced similar training with his team in Australia.

These were all behaviours that made him stand out for me as a leader. I am sometimes surprised when I am asked to run training for a leadership team, and the top leader fails to engage with me or the outcomes of the training, and will often fail to even attend themselves (too busy).

But what really made Chris shine in my eyes was what he did in the weeks and months after the training. Chris inspired his team to pick up the ball and run with it, and did a lot of work in the background to keep the new team agreements top of mind in the following months. But then he went beyond his team. He talked to his global leadership team, of which he was a member, and outlined what they had done, and the results they had achieved.

He shared the team agreements his team had produced with any of his peers who were interested in them, and made time to talk through them if necessary. He appointed internal champions to embed the productivity culture, and connected them with other teams if they needed help. Chris connected me with teams in London and Switzerland who were keen to boost their productivity, and bit by bit, we started to see the ripples that Chris was creating have a positive impact on more and more teams across the globe.

Chris was a busy man, but the inspiring thing was that he saw this drive for increased productivity across his organisation as a priority that he could lead. He did not wait for his boss to take the lead, he took affirmative action with his team, then inspired his peers to act as well. Chris recognised that productivity radiated out from himself, through his direct reports to his wider team,

Please don't wait for head office to put these initiatives in place. Be the change that you would like to see.

but did not stop there. He wanted that spiral to keep radiating out to touch as many of his colleagues as possible. He knew that productivity was a problem right across their very busy, very complex organisation, and he was in a position to do something positive to drive a change.

I have seen the same thing happen in other businesses too. Lesley Mackay, the general manager for Tasmania at the Smith Family, is an inspiring champion of productivity across her organisation. Steve Dastoli of Intralox has done some wonderful work with his team here in Australia and New Zealand, but has also championed the approach globally within his organisation. Maxim Sharshum at Medibank is another passionate productivity advocate within his organisation. These are busy people, but they see this work as above the line for them. They don't just approve the budget for the training, but lead from the front and get involved. I mention these few leaders here, but there are many, many more that I have worked with over the years. They are the exceptional ones, the elite ones!

Please don't wait for head office to put these initiatives in place. Be the change that you would like to see. That doesn't mean that you need to engage me or my team, or any external productivity experts to get started. It means that you need to make productivity a priority, for you and your team. It means going next level with your own personal productivity to start with. It means examining how you interface with your team to ensure that you create flow rather than friction. It means that you need to work on your team productivity cultures, and make it easier for your wider team to get their work done. And it means that you become an evangelist for productivity with your peers, colleagues and stakeholders (see figure 11.1).

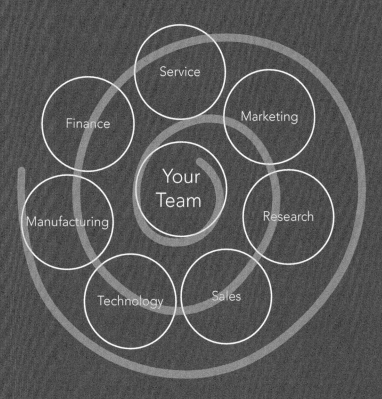

Figure 11.1: Productive organisation spiral

Share what you are doing—don't keep it a secret. Measure and share the results of the productivity initiatives you put in place. Instil a sense of pride within your team about their best-practice productivity approach, and tell the world about it. I love the quote that is attributed to JFK, amongst others: *'If not us, who? If not now, when?'*

In the introduction, I suggested that productivity was one of the strands in your leadership rope. It is a core strand, and your role as a leader, developing both the capability and capacity of your team, is one of the best uses of your time, energy and focus. All I hope is that you extend that rope to those around you and help them to climb to higher productivity heights.

Reflections and intentions

- What best-practice productivity strategies could you share with the external teams who interact with your team?

- What conversations could you have with your peers to put productivity on the agenda?

- Do you inspire your peers and their teams to work more productively with your team?

Conclusion

So, there it is, book number three in the Smart Productivity trilogy. *Smart Work* to enhance personal productivity, *Smart Teams* to help your team work better together, and *Lead Smart* to help you as a leader be the most productive leader you can be.

I hope that these three books, along with *Urgent!*, serve to inspire a different approach to productivity for you and your team, as well as deliver practical strategies that you can implement and benefit from. These books are nearly ten years in the making, and I believe they will stand the test of time. Technology will evolve, workplaces will change, but our friends, the Four Horsemen, will always be lurking just around the corner, waiting for an opportunity to disrupt our effectiveness. Busyness, Urgency, Disorganisation and Distraction never sleep, and we will always need to actively work against their insidious influence!

So, is that it? Maybe. I might put down the pen now and rest for a while. But I do have a quote on my office wall that I had framed after seeing an episode of *Grand Designs*, the British architectural show. The host Kevin McCloud asked a retired engineer if the house he had just designed and built was his last endeavour. The response was: *'I intend to have many busy years ahead. I have ideas in my head that I have not thought of yet.'*

I fear I may be the same. Bye for now.

adapt

Thank you for reading *Lead Smart*. With the advice in this book, you will be on the way to becoming the most productive leader you can be.

But your journey to being a better, smarter, more productive leader doesn't have to end here. If you feel that one of our speaking, training or coaching offerings could help to enhance your leadership and that of your team, get in touch through our website below, and let's make a time to talk.

www.adaptproductivity.com.au

I love connecting, so feel free to connect with me on LinkedIn or email me on

dermot@adaptproductivity.com.au

Until next time...

Dermot